CHOIR OF ANGELS

LINDA GUNTER

CHOIR OF ANGELS

Quantity sales special discounts are available on quantity purchases by corporations, associations, and others. For details, contact the publisher at the address above.

Orders by U.S. and Canada trade bookstores and wholesalers. Email info@ BeyondPublishing.net

The Beyond Publishing Speakers Bureau can bring authors to your live event. For more information or to book an event contact the Beyond Publishing Speakers Bureau speak@BeyondPublishing.net

The Author can be reached directly at info@BeyondPublishing.net

Manufactured and printed in the United States of America distributed globally by BeyondPublishing.net

BEYOND
PUBLISHING

New York | Los Angeles | London | Sydney

ISBN Hardcover: 978-1-637922-37-8

ISBN Softcover: 978-1-637922-38-5

TABLE OF CONTENTS

PREFACE

For years, my husband David and I kept ourselves incredibly busy, working tirelessly in the field of real estate investing in one of America's most vibrant cities, Atlanta. We built a prosperous business buying, restoring, and selling dozens of residential properties here in Georgia. It was the success of this very business alongside a divine encounter that set the stage for the start of our non-profit Love Him Love Them in 1998. Our first step with this ministry was to turn one of our residential properties – in the fifth worst crime ridden neighborhood in America, Vine City Atlanta – into a homeless shelter to respond to the tremendous need in that area. We named the shelter "George's Place," in honor of my father, Dr. George A. Schuler. As a privately funded shelter, we were able to teach our residents about Jesus alongside traditional vocational programs. Several years later, with new opportunities afoot, we moved to Northeast Georgia, where our real estate business and ministry expanded.

From time to time, friends would ask if David and I had any plans to have children and raise a family. To be honest, it was never anything I ever really envisioned. Actually, we made a deal on our very first date that we would never have children. We would soon learn the truth of that old expression, "If you want to make God laugh, tell Him your plans!" Nothing quite prepared me for the events that were to unfold, turning me into an "instant" mother of five, almost overnight!

A tragic event in 2004 changed our lives suddenly and dramatically. On October 30th of that year, I received a shocking call. A friend called to share the painful and disturbing news that our friend Myrna had been murdered earlier that day by her husband, leaving five children without a mother or father. By that time, we had known our delightful friend Myrna for several years, and often turned to her to handle mortgage arrangements for our real estate transactions. She had become a dear friend and confidante, and she had even asked me if I would serve as godmother to her youngest child.

Prior to meeting Myrna for the first time, I had given almost no thought to the Caribbean nation of Haiti, one of the most impoverished spots on the globe. I learned it was a place of oppressive poverty, even prior to the 2010 earthquake that nearly destroyed the island. Through my friendship with Myrna – following her death -- my connection to Haiti would change in a major way.

As we became friends, Myrna sought my advice on how she might arrange to bring her husband's two children from his prior marriage from Haiti to the U.S. Ultimately, they were successful in achieving that goal, and their family grew to include five children. For three years following Myrna's death, in his modest apartment in the Queens area of New York City, her elderly father did his best to care for the five children. David and I spoke with the children frequently, keeping the memory of their wonderful mother alive, and we made a point of sending gifts to the children several times each year for various holidays.

After one or two of Myrna's children returned to Georgia to spend a summer -- and then a full school year -- with us, it became clear that Myrna's father hoped that David and I would take the children. In 2007, that's exactly what David and I did, and we officially became a family of seven.

The number seven has special significance in the Bible – and scholars say that this number reflects "completeness" or "perfection." Following Creation, God rested on the seventh day – and there are numerous references to very important events that took place in the Bible on the seventeenth day of the seventh month, the same day we came together as a family of seven.

Four years later, as the Christmas holiday of 2011 rapidly approached, I proposed an idea to the other members of my family at one of our regular "family meetings." "What if," I asked, "instead of giving each of you the usual Christmas gifts, we use that money to travel to Haiti and spend the money we would normally spend on Christmas to help an orphanage." David and the children agreed that this would, indeed, make it a Christmas week like no other. After phone calls, airline bookings, and trip planning, we found ourselves in Haiti – where the extreme poverty and destruction visible everywhere we turned, less than two years after the devastating earthquake of January 2010, was truly disturbing.

Despite the challenges of simply meeting basic survival needs in Haiti, many of the people we met there were cheerful and welcoming – as well as courageous and inspiring. Many of the people we met on this trip have become embedded in our lives as ministry partners and valued friends. One of our greatest connections during this trip was meeting Pastor Maxeau, one of the few pastors on the ground in Haiti willing to host us during the week of Christmas. On Christmas Day, Pastor Maxeau invited us to his friend's orphanage called LifeSaver.

The 30 children who called the orphanage home sang for us, their voices united in angelic harmony. These children had nothing – no Christmas tree, no food, no water, no electricity, and no parents – but they clearly found joy in singing.

Having given out most gifts to an orphanage visited earlier that week, we were left with a suitcase of some sweet treats and flip-flops. Wishing we had more to give the children, we reluctantly opened our suitcase to hand out the ninety-nine cent flip flops. Miraculously, we happened to have precisely 30 pairs of flip-flops for the children -- the exact number and size that we needed! Wanting to help further, we pulled the orphanage's father, Pastor Paul, aside to ask after their greatest need. In response, we learned they had been praying for shoes for months, and our gift just answered their prayers and fulfilled their greatest need. That unexpected and miraculous turn of events inspired the title for my first book, "Peanut Butter Crackers and Flip-Flops" published in 2017. Our 2011 Christmas trip to Haiti made such a powerful impact on everyone in the family that this immediately became a very special annual tradition for us.

On that first visit to Haiti, I told Pastor Maxeau that someone needed to bring these beautiful and talented children to the U.S. to perform for audiences as the Haitian Orphan Children's Choir. With no disrespect, Pastor Maxeau replied that he had heard the same thing from every American who had visited the orphanage and heard the children sing – and yet no one was willing to do anything about it. I resolved that we would be the exception -- and five years later, the 30 children we met on Christmas Day at the LifeSaver Orphanage were traveling with me on a flight from Haiti to America for a nationwide concert tour. The money that we raised on the tour – through the truly beautiful concert performances that left audiences in tears -- enabled us to establish a home in Haiti where the children had food, water, and electricity -- a vast improvement over the way they had been living previously. As of today, 22 of the 30 children on that flight have had the opportunity to study in the U.S. on student visas, and some others are in the process of being adopted by American families.

As hundreds, perhaps thousands, of people have learned of the work of the Love Him Love Them Ministry, many of them have stepped forward and volunteered their time and skills in a wide variety of ways. Several years before I met her, one member of our team, Melinda, had worked with a group of children from Uganda, who similarly travelled to the U.S. to perform a series of concerts similar in nature to the performances we envisioned. Thanks to her work with the Uganda project, Melinda had experience working with the U.S. Homeland Security and knew how to handle the complicated paperwork needed to bring the children to the U.S. Miraculously, Melinda agreed to join our team, and she helped us obtain the travel visas the children needed.

Starting with that 2011 visit, celebrating the Christmas season with the orphans of Haiti each year has always been a profound experience for every member of the Love Him Love Them team. Each year, we make sure that each child in the orphanages, schools, and churches supported by our ministry receives a Christmas Joy Bag, a tradition the children have learned to eagerly anticipate.

One recent victory that I'm especially proud of – one that would never have been possible without money raised through concert performances by the Haitian Orphan Children's Choir and the generous donations received even when the choir was unable to tour– is the fact that we have been able to fund the construction of a desperately needed hospital in Haiti. This hospital opened its doors in 2020, despite the global pandemic.

The Love Him Love Them Ministry has grown in remarkable ways over the past two decades thanks to the extraordinary volunteers and donors, and today our organization partners with Feed the Hunger to feed 5,000 children in Haiti every day. Also, in addition to the medical facility opened in 2020, we have established six different locations in Haiti that include orphanages, schools, and churches. The Valley of Hope School established by the ministry offers K-through-13 classes, and for many of the children attending the school, the lunch they are served there is their only meal of the day. The children love attending school – and they truly appreciate their teachers, school uniforms and school supplies, in addition to the hot lunch.

Another learning center the ministry has established in Haiti includes the Vocational School, offering classes in nine different fields -- including computer skills, cooking, construction, cosmetology courses, and instruction in electrical work. Some of the students attending the vocational school think nothing of walking many miles to attend the school every day.

In addition, the Love Him Love Them ministry organizes several mission trips to Haiti every year, allowing dedicated volunteers from the U.S. an opportunity to help make a difference in the lives of children and families there.

The immigration challenges faced by orphans in Haiti have become more challenging than ever – especially at the time I write this preface. Once a girl or boy turns 18, they are no longer allowed to remain in an orphanage. Haitian immigration officials have recently rejected the visa applications we have prepared for orphans, in contrast to the approvals we had received in prior years, stating they are now more fearful than ever that the young people who leave the country will never return.

Rife with natural disaster, political instability, and violence, the level of tension in Haiti is currently higher than ever. On my most recent visit in May 2021, everyone seemed on edge due to recent kidnapping incidents and the resignation of the nation's Prime Minister. I've learned that many mission groups that had been working in Haiti since 2010 have now chosen to stay away because of the danger, but our ministry is more committed than ever to helping the children and families there.

We have encountered many challenges along the way – as you will read in the pages that follow – and often we feel as if there is no possible solution. At those moments, we hold onto the truth of Habakkuk 3:18-19 (Amplified Bible):

Yet I will [choose to] rejoice in the LORD; I will [choose to] shout in exultation in the [victorious] God of my salvation! The Lord GOD is my strength [my source of courage, my invincible army]; He has made my feet [steady and sure] like hinds' feet And makes me walk [forward with spiritual confidence] on my high places [of challenge and responsibility].

Then we roll up our sleeves and get back to work. It continues to be the most rewarding work of my life, and I can't wait to tell you all about it! (As you will see, we have learned to expect miracles!)

Let's begin!

Linda Gunter

Atlanta, Georgia

June 2021

CHOIR OF
ANGELS

INTRODUCTION

CHAPTER ONE

Jeremiah 29:11

"For I know the plans I have for you," declares the Lord,
"plans to prosper you and not to harm you, plans to give
you hope and a future.

E very one of us can look back through our lives and identify a set of markers that changed the trajectory of our lives moving forward. As I walk down memory lane to share my journey with you, every one of those experiences have served as a marker on the path that has propelled me onto the personal and professional path that I walk today. Some of those experiences were welcome moments of joy, where I could easily declare words of thanks and praise to the Lord for his overwhelming goodness in my life. Others were moments of great struggle, where I had to wade through the swamp of frustration, heartbreak, and hopelessness, so I could refocus my eyes back on the Lord. For all these moments, whether full of joy or of struggle, I have learned the strength of faith that comes with a focus set solely on the Lord.

Jeremiah 29:11 offers us a beautiful and well-known promise from the Lord. He promises his plans are to prosper us with a promised hope and future. It's in that same scripture, verse 12 – 14, that we're instructed to call on him and come and pray to him, and then he will listen. "'I will be found by you,' declares the Lord, and will bring you back from captivity.'" When facing difficult circumstances, it's easy to tumble down into the pit of despair and heartache. It's easy to fall prey to the captivity of anxious thoughts. It's easy to clothe ourselves with an identity of failure. It's easy to entertain the temptation of giving up. Having lost my best friend Myrna to the brutal circumstance of murder, I've known the pit of despair. Having fostered and cared for her five children as they struggled with and questioned the loss of their mother, father, and grandmother in one fell swoop, I've known how it feels to want to give up. I've shared their anger. Having fervently prayed for healing over another best friend who lost her life to the bitter disease of cancer, I've known the feeling of failure. Having walked through many bleak circumstances with outcomes fully unknown, the Lord has used the path set before me to develop in me an intimate understanding of faith. I've learned how to find that often elusive sense of hope in the Lord's promises. I've learned to look back on those times in my life, those past markers, where the Lord has delivered me time and time again through seemingly insurmountable circumstances to places I'd never even thought to ask for or imagine.

Many readers first learned how my husband David and I established the Love Him Love Them Ministry when they read my first book, "Peanut Butter Crackers and Flip Flops," published four years ago. In that book, I share the story of how our family grew, almost overnight, from the two of us to a busy household of seven. It's worth noting that we grew to a family of seven on the 17th day of the seventh month of the year 2007, with children ranging in age from seven to 17. As I noted earlier, the number seven has special significance in the Bible. It is a number that reflects "completeness" or "perfection."

In that book, we closed with the details of how we were able to bring 30 beautiful and talented orphans to the United States for a concert tour in 2016. We had just received the approval for 30 visas in order to bring an orphanage of Haitian children to the United States to sing. Never could we have imagined where that path would lead us. God chose our family and ministry to be His hands and feet, to be His conduit to provide miracles for children that the earthquake of 2010 in Haiti left behind. I couldn't have imagined the spiritual trial or heartbreak I would come to experience. Nor could I have anticipated the unbridled joy, spiritual growth, and strength of faith that this journey would soon bring. With steadfast focus on the Lord, strength of faith, and a response of "Yes, Lord!" to the ministry in which we'd been called, our journey begins.

THEY JUST PUT MAGINE
IN AN AMBULANCE

C H A P T E R   T W O

Romans 8:29

And we know that in all things God works for the good of those who love him, who have been called according to his purpose.

They just put Magine in an ambulance," were the words I heard as soon as I answered the phone call from Daddy Chase at the choir house. "She is having convulsions and her fever is sky high. We've done everything we know to do, and as far as I know, they are taking her to the hospital in Anderson" a small town not far from Greenville, South Carolina.

Magine, at four years of age, was the youngest child I met at the LifeSaver orphanage in Haiti, on an unforgettable Christmas Day in 2011. After a long journey of endless paperwork, embassy interviews and financial hurdles, all 30 of the children from her Haitian orphanage were now in the United States. I met Magine for the first time when she was only four months old. She had been dropped off at the Haitian orphanage along with her older sister, Seyma, by an aunt. Their father had died, and their aunt was unable to provide care for the girls. The orphanage did their best to explain to the aunt they lacked the diapers, bottles, cribs and other items required to properly care for an infant. After the girls' aunt begged the orphanage to keep Magine for just 24 hours to give her time to make other arrangements for the baby, the orphanage reluctantly agreed. They never saw the girls' aunt again. The girls were dropped at the orphanage three weeks before my first trip to Haiti. It was Christmas 2011 when I cradled the beautiful four-month-old baby in my arms, sitting on a urine-stained daybed, as a group of orphans sang to me, a moment that changed the trajectory of my life forever.

Linda and Magine sitting on the urine-stained Day Bed the first time they met December 25, 2011

Now my beautiful Magine was four years old and, after having been in America for only one week, I was shocked to learn that she was in an ambulance on the way to a hospital emergency room. Sitting in the car with my husband David, I put my phone down and shared this troubling news with him. David immediately made a U-turn and pressed on the accelerator, as we sped to meet the ambulance carrying this precious baby at the hospital.

With our hearts racing with panic and worry, I did the only thing available to me at that time… I prayed. As David and I raced to the hospital, I prayed the only way I knew how, asking the Lord to help us! I told God this was not what was supposed to happen. We didn't bring this precious child to America for her to die! Arriving at the hospital moments after the ambulance, tears were flooding down my face as I watched as paramedics rapidly carried Magine, who lay motionless on a stretcher, into the Emergency Room.

Gertrude and Paul, the mother and papa of the LifeSaver orphanage in Haiti, where we had first met Magine and 29 other boys and girls, had accompanied the children on their visit to America for their first choir tour. They were living with the children in the choir house, to help with their care. As Magine was loaded into the ambulance at the choir house, Gertrude accompanied the young girl on her way to the emergency room. Gertrude spoke no English, and – at that time – I had very little comprehension of Creole (the national language of Haiti), so there were many questions being asked about this medical emergency, but no one really had any idea of Magine's condition. Regardless of the language barrier, both Gertrude and I -- as mother figures to this beautiful little girl – both felt a deep sense of anticipation and concern. As hospital personnel frantically clustered around the three of us in the middle of the hospital lobby, attempting to get information from us about Magine, confusion reigned. While the nursing staff was trying to figure out who was whom and the role we each played in this precious child's life, Magine lay -- dripping sweat on a gurney, in an extremely lethargic state.

Shortly after arrival, with our interpreter in tow, we were taken to a room in the ER. A nurse stepped in the room, introducing herself as Amy Jo. She immediately assessed Magine's condition, while scanning all the people in the room. She very politely, but sternly, asked, "Okay, what's the story here?" As I began to reply, she interrupted me to ask, "What language are you all speaking?" It was hospital procedure to setup a landline phone to dial in an interpreter for patients who did not speak English. As another nurse was connecting the phone, I answered, "Creole, Haitian Creole." Although we had an interpreter with us, the hospital staff attempted to reach their own interpreter by phone, as their standards required. Ultimately unsuccessful in reaching anyone, our own interpreter, in person, took over. As the nursing staff took blood and setup IV fluids to re-hydrate Magine, we sat around her bed praying and asking God to bring healing. The final doctor's report identified Magine's ailment as a febral seizure, a very common and treatable condition. The doctor assured us, "Don't worry, it will probably never happen again."

As we waited for Magine to be released from the ER, David walked out of the room and to our car to retrieve a business card and a copy of our book, "Peanut Butter Crackers and Flip Flops," to give the hospital staff. I autographed the book, including my cell phone number, and gave it to Amy Jo, the sweet nurse who had been so kind to us during our four hours in the emergency room.

David and I left the hospital with Magine, and we sent everyone else back to the choir house. Magine slept during the entire one-hour drive to our home, including a stop at Walmart to fill her prescription and to purchase enough clothing for her to survive a few days of treasured time at Mommy Linda's house ("Mommy Linda" being the name affectionately given to me by the choir).

Two days later, I received a phone call from Amy Jo, the kind ER nurse who cared for us during Magine's visit to the emergency room. Amy Jo's voice was cracking on the phone, and she had obviously been crying. She began by explaining that she was a life flight nurse and very seldom worked there in the ER. Amy Jo said that she felt it was a divine intervention and a miracle that she was there in the ER when we arrived. With a voice still cracking, Amy Jo said, "I read the book you gave me at the hospital, and I was completely overwhelmed by your story. I am calling to ask you how I can become involved with what you are doing and how I can help you. And, of course, I wanted to check on Magine."

Magine's trip to the ER resulted in opening an amazing door for us with Amy Jo. I responded by saying, "We actually have a boy named Eldo, who has been raised in the same orphanage in Haiti as Magine. He was born with six fingers on each hand." I explained to Amy Jo that, in Haiti, a condition like this carried the horrible stigma of being cursed, often leading to immediate rejection. I let Amy Jo know, "We are hoping to find a plastic surgeon or someone in America who can help him." "Consider it done!" Amy Jo answered back. "I'll make some calls tomorrow and get back to you." We excitedly said our good-byes.

When you meet as many people as I do, you constantly hear the phrase, "I can help you with that and I'll get back in touch with you." Many other times, you hear no assurances at all. My mother always told me that one very simple way you can stand out in this world is to "*Do* what you say you are going to do, and *don't do* what you say you are *not* going to do." Not many people do that. Twelve days passed after Amy Jo's heartfelt phone call. Then I received a text from her, saying, "Hey, it's Amy Jo. Call Dr. Terrence Bruner at this number, I've already spoken with his office and they are happy to do the surgery for the young boy we spoke about." I just stared at my phone with tears streaming down my face. One phone call to Dr. Bruner's office led to scheduling an appointment with him. Before we knew it, we were in the doctor's viewing suite, watching the surgery to remove the 2 extra fingers from Eldo's hands.

Whenever I reflect on Dr. Bruner's surgery, transforming the boy's life, I am always reminded of several promotional photos of the orphan's choir that include Eldo, especially a huge photo of the group gathered in the back of the tour bus we used for our concert tours. In these photos, Eldo's hands can always be seen, extending up in the air praising Jesus. In each photo, you can clearly see the extra finger on each of his hands, and despite the rejection and stigma his condition created, Eldo always radiated joy. Dr. Bruner's surgery was a gift to him, and Amy Jo was a gift to us. A gift we never would have received without that trip to the emergency room with Magine.

Picture on the back of the Love Him Love Them choir tour bus

Amy Jo and Dr. Bruner. The 2 angels who worked together to make the dream of Eldo's surgery a reality

Mommy Linda presenting Amy Jo with a Love Him Love Them Haitian orphan choir CD as a small token of thanks for all she did to help us with Eldo's surgery

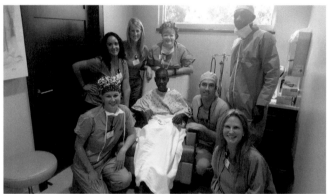

Eldo and Dr. Bruner's amazing staff that made Eldo's dream come true

Eldo and Mommy Macarena just before Eldo's surgery

MICHELINE AND THE FIRST TIME

CHAPTER THREE

1 John 4:4

You, dear children, are from God and have overcome them, because the one who is in you is greater than the one who is in the world.

One day, as we were back on the road heading for the next destination on our concert tour, I heard more ruckus than usual as I sat behind the wheel, driving the bus. I looked in the rearview mirror, and I could see four or five children gathered in the aisle of the bus, standing over another one of the children. Then I heard one of the children say, "She's not breathing!" I tried to get the attention of another one of the children, to understand what was happening. Out of the corner of the mirror, I could see Paul William, the papa of the LifeSaver orphanage in Haiti. He was sitting completely still, facing forward, and looking directly ahead, even though the commotion was taking place approximately two rows behind him, in the aisle. I thought his behavior, under these disturbing circumstances, was very strange. As the screaming continued to get louder, I pulled the bus off the interstate, and onto the next exit ramp. I jumped out of my seat and made it down the bus aisle, navigating my way through all the kids piled together, to the source of the commotion. I looked down on the floor, and in the aisle of the bus I saw one of the girls, Micheline, convulsing and unconscious. With my heart in my stomach, I ran back to the front of the bus to get my phone to dial 911 while simultaneously checking for the closest hospital on my phone. I was screaming the whole time to the back of the bus, "Is she ok? Is she still breathing?" All the while, I could still see Paul William in the mirror, not budging, sitting seemingly unfazed and unconcerned. I couldn't understand his strange, passive behavior. Why wasn't he on the floor trying to save Micheline's life?

Hopping back into the driver's seat of the bus, I looked up and saw a CVS sign right around the corner. I yelled for the kids to take their seats, stepped on the accelerator, and raced into the CVS parking lot on what felt like two wheels. I jumped out of the bus, hoping to find a nurse, pharmacist, medic or ANYONE who could help me. One of the older boys jumped off the bus trailing me, and as we were running across the parking lot, he yelled to me, "Mommy Linda, you do know that what's happening to Micheline is from a demon, right?" I almost tripped over my feet as I came to a quick halt. I stared at the boy like he was crazy, but no words came out of my mouth. He continued to explain, "It's voodoo." With a shake of my head and the plea on my tongue that Micheline needed medical help, I left him and ran inside CVS. Yelling for a nurse or pharmacist, I screamed, "I have an unconscious child on the bus." A lady came running from behind the pharmacy counter with a stethoscope and some other medical monitoring devices. All the while, my thoughts were racing with what

I had just learned about the attack being "voodoo." I ran with the nurse across the parking lot toward the bus, explaining what happened and preparing her for what she was about to see. Her sole focus was on making it to the bus, and apparently was not giving much thought to my explanation. As soon as we boarded the bus, we moved the kids out of the way and made it to where Micheline was laying on the floor, now awake and responsive. The CVS nurse pulled out the monitoring devices she had with her, and leaned over and began to measure Micheline's vitals signs. Then she stood up and said, "Her vital signs are normal. She's fine!"

The CVS nurse got off the bus, and we walked back to the entrance of the drugstore. I kept asking the nurse to give me some sense of what was wrong with Micheline. She said, "She's fine, maybe she was just trying to get some attention." I lowered my head and quietly said, almost in a whisper, "These children on the bus are from Haiti, they mentioned to me that this could be some sort of voodoo spell that caused this. Is that possible?" The nurse looked at me like I was an alien, and said, "The girl is fine." Not knowing what else to do or say, I thanked her and got back on the bus.

I drove the bus out of the CVS parking lot and got back on the interstate. My heart was beating so hard and fast I felt like it was going to explode. My mind kept circling around the thoughts, "What happened to her? What caused this? What if she had died?" Before we even reached the next exit, I pulled the bus over to the side of the interstate. With a fortified spirit and conviction regarding what I had to do, I stood in the aisle of the bus and with tears streaming down my face. I asked our interpreter (the only person on the bus who knew both English and Creole) to join me as we presented the gospel to everyone on the bus. As the bus sat on the side of the interstate, eight children prayed to receive Jesus as their Lord and Savior. I was holding onto the only assurance I had, in the midst of the strange and confusing incident we had just experienced, and that assurance was that GREATER is HE that is in me than he that is in the world. Those eight children who received Jesus that day were all baptized a few weeks later, during a visit to the beaches of South Carolina's Edisto Island.

I had no idea what happened to Micheline that day. It took a long time for me to even begin to understand anything that happened on that strange day. However, Paul William, the papa of the orphanage – who had been so passive during this strange incident -- knew EXACTLY what was happening. He had witnessed incidents like this time and time again at the orphanage in Haiti. Instead of reaching out for medical help for Micheline, he was battling in the spiritual realm to help her, something that would take me years to understand or even begin to figure out!

TONY HOLTZCLAW
STUCK IN VALDOSTA / STUCK IN AMERICA

CHAPTER FOUR

Luke 6:38

Give, and it will be given to you. A good measure, pressed down,
shaken together and running over, will be poured into your lap.
For with the measure you use, it will be measured to you.

In October of 2016, we were heading for Tamarac, Florida – just north of Ft. Lauderdale – the site of our final concert on the orphans' first tour. The children were scheduled to perform at a Haitian church there in Tamarac. We were working our way down to south Florida, en route to Miami, where we'd catch our flight back home to Haiti. While on stage for the concert, I had my cell phone in my back pocket, set to vibrate. (I never wanted my phone to ring during a performance, disrupting the experience for our audience.) After the third song of our choir performance, I was on stage introducing the kids when the phone in my back pocket started vibrating. With calls, emails and texts coming in constantly throughout the day, at first, I didn't think much about receiving yet another call --- but my phone just kept on vibrating and vibrating.

We had 30 reservations with Delta – one for each of the children -- and each one listed me as the person to contact in the event of any emergency. We were all scheduled to take a Delta flight from Miami to Haiti the next morning, and the airline had cancelled the flight because Hurricane Matthew was rapidly approaching the island. After introducing the children, I came offstage and pulled my phone out of my pocket, to see what was going on. There it was, plain as day, 30 times over… YOUR FLIGHT HAS BEEN CANCELLED. THERE ARE NO OTHER ARRANGEMENTS BEING MADE AT THIS TIME. NO FLIGHTS INTO HAITI UNTIL FURTHER NOTICE. I quietly put my phone down on the pew and went back up and finished the concert.

Throughout the rest of the concert, my mind was racing. Where will we go? What will we do? How long could we stay here? We had host families for the night, but I had no idea where we were and didn't know a soul in this town. Our plan had been to stay with our host families for the evening, and then everyone would be dropped off at the church the next morning. We'd load onto the bus and travel to the airport together. I was going to leave the bus at the Miami airport and then, after getting the kids settled back in Haiti, catch a return flight to Miami to pick the bus back up and drive it back home. My tour companion, Macarena, who accompanied us throughout the tour, to help care for the kids, drove the Love Him Love Them van with overflow space for the children, musical instruments, and items for sale at our product table. Macarena was planning to drive the van and the trailer back home to Lavonia, Georgia as soon as the children and I had safely boarded our flight. I had no idea what to do. Because the choir was performing in a Haitian church, by the time we wrapped up the concert, everyone except our choir moms, Macarena and our kids knew there was a major hurricane headed to Haiti – as most audience members had been in touch with relatives who told them about the approaching storm.

With the kids already being drawn to the amazing aroma of the Haitian food waiting for them in the small fellowship hall, following their performance, they raced off out of the sanctuary while I held the musicians back. I told them a hurricane was on the way to Haiti, and our flights had been cancelled. With an understanding of just how dangerous hurricanes in Haiti could be, our drummer immediately said we needed to pray now for everyone in Haiti, and we did. We stopped and prayed for their families, the orphanages, their friends, their schools, their churches… really for everything. When we were finished, the peace of prayer quickly eroded to confusion when I told them we might be stuck in the United States for a day, a week, or a month… we didn't really know when we'd be able to return to Haiti. With the children's visas due to expire in three days, we'd likely be illegally overstaying our visas in the United States. Their faces all changed, and everyone was perplexed.

The musicians started tearing down their instruments and equipment on the stage of the church, and I went to find the pastor. He was already gone. In lieu of talking with the pastor, I met with a lady from the church who had made all the arrangements for our host families. Although everyone at the church knew Hurricane Michael was rapidly heading towards Haiti, no one fully understood how it would affect the 30 children eating in their fellowship hall, and no one knew how it might affect the host families. Would they be stuck with us for the next few days? Longer?

Not yet mentioning this unexpected circumstance to any of the kids, I went home with my host family, where I spent much of the night on the phone with Delta, trying to figure out what to do. To add insult to injury, I was there at my host family's home without the bus, because as we were leaving the church, it would not start.

The next morning, I called my contact at the Homeland Security department in Washington, to find out if there was anything we could do to extend the children's Visas. I then called every other airline with service to Haiti, to see if we could move our reservations to another flight. Because of the approaching hurricane, all flights into Haiti had been cancelled, and no one knew how long it would be until flights would once again be operating in Haiti.

In the meantime, we arranged for a tow truck to bring our bus to the garage of a mechanic who was friends with one of the church members. While the kids were waiting at the church, having been dropped off by their host families at the scheduled meeting time, one of the church members gave me a ride to the garage where the bus was being fixed. We were at a standstill. The kids stayed at the church for a couple of hours, but quickly became restless with nothing to do. Using our Love Him Love Them van and the vehicles of the members and staff, the kids were driven over to the garage where I was waiting for the bus to be repaired.

Can you imagine 30 kids hanging around a mechanic's garage? All 30 kids were "hanging out in the bus" that wouldn't start. There was no air conditioning, no way to occupy them with a movie, and seemingly no way to entertain these restless children. We were also beginning to feel the effect of the hot temperatures of South Florida. In desperation, I noticed there was a Dunkin Donuts shop right next to the mechanic's garage, so I began taking kids to get donuts, one group of four at a time. When I appeared with a group of children for the third time, the owner of the donut shop and his wife couldn't resist asking what was going on. "Who are all these children?," they asked. I shared our story.

The owner of the donut shop mentioned that he was Muslim, and wanted to know if, being a Christian ministry, it would be okay if he paid for all the children's donuts and gave us an additional $100.00. You can imagine my response to that question! At that point, I brought all of the children in, and we crowded into the tiny donut shop and sang two songs. We also briefly told the owner and his wife, and a few of their customers, about our story, and the result was plenty of tears over the donuts.

Our unexpected adventure in Tamarac continued to unfold. The mechanic let me know that a part had to be ordered, to repair the bus. Someone from the church realized we were still in town and cooked a delicious Haitian lunch for us. A few members of the church brought the meal over to the garage for us, and then -- realizing how hot it was outside -- carpooled the kids back to the church to eat. The essential part for the bus repair finally came in, and I was able to drive it back to the church later that afternoon, where 30 restless children were waiting, coloring, sleeping on pews, and running around. I still had not received any word from our contact at Homeland Security, regarding extending the children's visas because of the hurricane. After speaking with my husband David, we made the decision that the smartest thing for us to do was to head back to Georgia – with the whole group -- where we had resources, connections, and people who could help.

Having already packed up and returned the keys to choir house for the end of our summer tour, we were left without our usual food supply or beds or choir bookings. Stranded in the US with no idea when we'd be able to head back to Haiti, we began our drive north to Georgia. Not wanting to miss a good public relations opportunity, I began to contact every news media outlet I could think of, to share the story of the "Haitian Orphan Children's Choir stranded in the US, unable to return to Haiti due to Hurricane Michael." The plan was to drive until we couldn't physically drive any longer, and then David would help us find hotel rooms, to rest our heads that evening.

After a 400-mile drive, we crossed the Georgia border and made it to a town just south of Valdosta. At that point, our colleague Macarena called and said the van "sounded funny." We pulled off on the side of the interstate and made another call to David as we tried to figure out what to do. After a long conversation and a lot of poking and prodding around the van's engine compartment, it became clear that the van wasn't going any further that night. By this time, it was already dark, and the kids were complaining they were hungry. I called another tow truck, a skill that was starting to become "second nature" for me! We moved all of our belongings and countless children into the bus, and we sat and waited for the tow truck to arrive. Our van was pulling a trailer, and the tow truck driver balked at towing both – so we just left our trailer on the side of the road. By the time we were finally able to head towards a hotel, it was very late into the night.

We found a Holiday Inn Express in Valdosta and planned how many people we'd put into each room. I decided to bunk with six of our choir girls. After making sure that everyone in our big group was all set for the night, I headed back to the room I was sharing with the girls. To say I was exhausted would be an understatement. Aside from the minor annoyance of walking into a smoke-filled hotel room with the six girls just sitting around as the fire alarm was going off, it was a restful night. I learned that one of our girls, Samaika, had decided to make popcorn in the microwave but left it in for too long – and the bag had caught fire. Unconcerned, the girls remained sitting on the bed as the alarm blared. Needless to say, there was never a dull moment. What a day!

The next morning, we got our full "money's worth" from the hotel's free breakfast buffet. As the kids swam in the hotel's swimming pool, we found a garage to look at the van. When I reached out to a high school friend who ran the YMCA in Valdosta, she brought us some Chick-fil-A cards for lunch. However, after the 30 of us entered the Chick-fil-A and ordered our lunch, we naturally received questions about the kids, which was normal in a crowd our size. When we shared our story and the kids sang at the restaurant, the Chick-fil-A manager generously gave us our lunch for free, returning the Chick-fil-A gift cards back for us to use another time.

At Chic-fil-a in Valdosta, Georgia with high school friend Cheryl Marshall right after being treated to lunch for singing.

After lunch, we received a call from the garage that had been working on our van. The gentleman I spoke with said the cost of repairing the van far exceeded the value of the van – and, as a result, it wasn't worth fixing. I had no idea what to do. We were still waiting for our flights to Haiti to be rescheduled, the children's visas were due to expire in two days, and we had no van to go get the trailer sitting on the side of the interstate, which contained all of our musical instruments and luggage. Now clearly in "Emergency Mode," I turned to social media and posted a Facebook Live video, updating our followers, to see if there was anyone out there who might be able to help. A few minutes later, I got a call.

The call was from Tony Holtzclaw, the pastor from Harmony Baptist Church in Dawsonville, Georgia – and he said the most precious words! "Linda, we are on our way. We have a tow bed, so we'll pick up the van from the mechanic and bring it here. Then we can decide what to do with it. I have another bus at the church we can bring along to transport the kids that were riding in the van, and we have a truck that can pull the trailer. See you in about four hours." I just put the phone down, took a breath and cried tears of relief. I went to the front desk to ask for a late check out, and then went to the pool where our children were once again playing. I sat at a table marveling at the fact that, apparently, our Haitian children didn't have a care in the world, splashing around in water having the time of their lives while water from a hurricane was completely devastating their country.

Everything Tony said on the phone call came to pass. Five hours later, we were loading up children on buses and headed back to... well, we weren't sure where! We stopped for dinner along the way, and

Tony told me that his church was preparing their gym, as a place for us to stay, for as long as we needed. They were putting out air mattresses for all of us, and they would provide us with meals and whatever else we needed until we were able to fly back to Haiti. He said we could do another concert at his church, and continue to use his church vehicles for as long as we needed. In that moment, no sweeter words of assurance could have been spoken to me.

Before we arrived at the church, a lady named Lynn, who owned a garage near Harmony Baptist Church, called and said she would come and get our van from Tony's church and make the needed repairs free of charge. When we finally arrived at Tony's church, there was an incredible welcoming committee and more food than you can imagine. As the days passed, television stations and radio stations and newspaper reporters showed up daily to get updates on the kids and find out what we needed or how the community could help. We were literally on every news station in Atlanta. The kids had games to play, during their days at Harmony Baptist, and were taken to a high school football game, where of course they sang the National Anthem. By this point, all our choir moms and dads had other obligations since, technically, the tour was over. It was just me. Finally, David and I ended up taking shifts staying with the kids. It was CRAZY!

When we sang at the football game this fabulous rainbow appeared right above us!)

We waited daily to hear ANYTHING from the airlines or Homeland Security. We found out the only way to extend visas was to have applied for extensions months earlier. No matter what options were available, none of them worked. We were going to have the black mark of overextending the stay on our visas – regardless of the hurricane. There was nothing else that could be done -- so, we WAITED. We kept getting reports of the terrible devastation left in Hurricane Matthew's path over Haiti, and then finally, the coast was clear. Seven days later, we boarded the plane to return to Haiti.

When we returned to Haiti, it was as if there was a wall of protection around our ministries in Haiti. Miraculously, not one person or one building – school, church, orphanage -- had any damage. That, however, was not true for the rest of the country. It was a hot mess. There were signs of the hurricane's destructive power everywhere we turned.

What Tony Holtzclaw and his congregation did for us there in Valdosta was unprecedented, despite the fact that it was a modest church. No matter what child in the choir you ask, every one of them will give you the same response to the simple question, "Of all the places you sang, during all three choir tours, what was your favorite church?" You guessed it... the answer is HARMONY BAPTIST every time! We will always be eternally grateful.

Tony Holtzclaw and his twin from the lifesaver orphanage Gerson

Mommy Linda with Wendy Corona and cameraman from WSB -Channel 2 just after interview with the choir about being "Stranded in America" because of Hurricane Michael

Mommy Linda and reporter from Fox 5 Atlanta who fell in love with Zakary just after interviewing him about how it feels to not be able to go back to Haiti because of Hurricane Michael)

Daddy Chase (Choir intern) setting up beds on Harmony Baptist gym floor,
Our new home until we were able to fly back to Haiti

Harmony Baptist coming to the rescue to tow the van for us

BIANCA THROWING HERSELF OFF THE BUS

CHAPTER FIVE

Ephesians 6:12

For our struggle is not against flesh and blood, but against the rulers, against the authorities, against the powers of this dark world and against the spiritual forces of evil in the heavenly realms.

Back on the road again for a second summer season touring with our Haitian Orphan Choir, we were thrilled to have a full schedule that frequently kept us on the road. With a performance scheduled most weekdays, and two or more frequently scheduled for Saturday or Sunday, our tour bus quickly became the second home on wheels – for our children, and for me -- throughout the course of the choir tour. We found ourselves once again on the bus, navigating our way to another church that was hosting us for the evening, giving us a place to rest our heads in between performances. As often happens, travelling with 30 children, we were running behind schedule. With the sun having already set just beyond the horizon and the sky darkening quickly, I made a phone call to the church to let them know we were running late. The children, unfazed by our tardiness, were enjoying their time together in the back of the bus. The sounds of singing, talking, and activity carried their way to me as I drove to the church a little faster than normal, trying to make up for lost time.

Well into our drive, Alana, a college-aged volunteer who was serving with our ministry that summer as our "choir mom," made her way from the back to the front of the bus to inform me that one of our girls, Bianca, was sick. By this time in our choir tour, we had experienced multiple confusing situations with Bianca. Situations that were not normal. Situations that we would slowly come to realize were demonic manifestations. The word "sick" had become our code word to communicate that there may be something more happening than your general physical ailment, as the world would understand it. Alana explained that she, our musicians, and some of the other children had been praying over Bianca, and holding her down for over an hour. Alana said that things had just calmed down enough to give her a chance to come up and tell me about the incident. I asked Alana if I should stop the bus, and she told me she felt like everything was calming down and not to worry. As Alana headed back to her seat in the back of the bus, I continued driving, albeit with a closer eye on the rearview mirror. Just as Alana indicated, everyone seemed to be calming down, and within 30 minutes, everything appeared to be fully back to normal. Well, I guess the word "normal" is relative. But let's just say it was as "normal" as one would expect driving down a highway with 30 children onboard!

The next time I looked in my rearview mirror, I saw Bianca walking up the aisle toward me and the front of the bus. Strangely, the closer she came to me, the faster she was walking. The next thing I heard was Alana screaming, "Get her! Get her! That's not Bianca! Get her!" Two of the musicians sitting closest to me jumped over the seats and landed on top of Bianca just as she tried to jump through the large glass door at the front of the bus. Alana was running toward the front of the bus crying out, "Bianca said she needed to throw something away, I didn't think anything about it until she was halfway up here!" The trash can on the bus was located right beside the big glass door.

As the two musicians who were holding Bianca were attempting to carry her back to a seat so they could lay her down and prevent her from trying anything dangerous, I eased the bus to the side of the highway. With my heart in my stomach, I pulled myself out of the driver's seat and turned to see the two musicians holding an unconscious Bianca. With one more incident to add to our growing list of strange behaviors, I had begun to accept the truth that what I was facing was more than flesh and blood. I asked all of the kids to settle down and take their seats, and I took a deep breath to calm my beating heart. Then I pulled out my phone and began dialing the number to the pastor of the church hosting us that evening. I explained to the pastor that one of our children just tried to jump through a glass door on the bus while we were traveling 75 miles an hour down the interstate. I told the pastor that Bianca was thankfully on the bus, but currently unconscious, and we were still over an hour away. My next words were softly spoken. "It is a spiritual attack." The pastor instructed me to get to the church as quickly as possible with the assurance that he would have people praying while we were en route.

Back in the driver's seat, I once again started up the ignition and merged back onto the highway. en route to the church while Alana remained in the back of the bus to watch over Bianca. During the entirety of that hour spent on the road, I prayed to God, asking for help, asking Him to keep us safe. I couldn't stop looking over to that glass door, each time shivering with chills. The only comfort during that drive were the two strong boys we posted at the front of the bus near the glass door to prevent any further escape attempts. It was those two boys, my guardian angels, over the next sixty minutes, who gave me the strength to continue, on course. Needless to say, no one was allowed to use the trash can for the rest of the night.

We arrived at the church and drove around to the back entrance, as instructed. With grateful eyes I saw the pastor and several other church members waiting for us outside the church. I jumped out of the driver's seat and exited the bus. From behind, I heard Alana repeating "I knew that wasn't her going to the trash can, I shouldn't have let her trick me like that! This dang girl tried to throw herself off this bus! I knew that wasn't her!"

I nervously watched as Alana and two of the musicians carried Bianca off the bus through the same glass door she tried to jump out of earlier in our trip. In a semiconscious state, Bianca had her hands around her neck attempting to strangle herself. Upon exiting the bus, the two musicians kept hold of Bianca while at the same time trying to keep her hands from circling too tightly around her neck.

As her aggression subsided, the pastor from the church instructed the musicians to stop carrying Bianca and to make her walk by herself. They just looked at him skeptically, and kept carrying her. Then the pastor again suggested they put her down and let her walk by herself. Knowing Bianca couldn't walk by her own faculty, but desperately wanting to see Bianca freed from what they knew to be a demonic hold, the musicians laid her down. She just laid limp on the concrete under the awning leading into the church. The pastor and two of his church members picked her up with care and took her the rest of the way into the church. Dency, our piano player, and I followed them into the sanctuary, while Alana, the remaining church members, and the rest of the choir, including the two boys who had helped to carry Bianca off the bus, had disappeared in pursuit of the food that was being served. The pastor kindly told me and Dency we could both leave and go eat while they cared for Bianca but knowing and having experienced not only the unpredictability of the attacks, but the brute strength that could manifest within a child under attack, we chose to stay and help.

As Dency and I watched, the pastor and his team kept repeating Bianca's name, trying to get a response. The pastor asked one of his members to retrieve the olive oil from the remembrance table, located right above where Bianca was laying on the floor at the front of the church. They took the anointing oil and poured some on her forehead. He continued to call out her name. They prayed over her, speaking and praying in tongues by the gifting of the Holy Spirit. As Dency and I looked on, they would periodically stop and ask us questions. "How long has this been happening?" "How long has she been like this?" All the while Bianca was just lying there totally unresponsive. They continued praying and put more oil on her body, and about 30 minutes later, Bianca sat up, looking a little groggy. Covered in self-inflicted scratch marks on her face and neck, she asked me where all the children were and wanted to know if she could go get something to eat. She had no recollection of anything that had occurred over the last three and a half hours.

Thankful and relieved to see her fully conscious and self-aware, Dency directed Bianca out of the sanctuary and into the room where dinner was being served. I stayed with the Pastor, knowing there'd undoubtedly be questions about everything that had transpired that evening. I did my best to explain what had happened. He asked me if Bianca had ever been anointed with oil. I was sure she had, but I couldn't really remember an exact moment, so I didn't really answer in the affirmative. All I could think was that I was glad they had only seen the last 30 minutes of a three and a half hour ordeal. Having seen a mostly unconscious Bianca during the 30 minutes under his care, I wondered what he would do or say if he had seen everything that had happened on the bus. However, out of my own fear of the response I might get, knowing how unbelievable everything might appear, I kept my mouth shut, which some would say is unusual for me.

The kind members of the church had set up air mattresses for all of us to sleep on the floor of their fellowship hall. Physically and mentally exhausted from the day's ordeals, I went in, blew up my air mattress and fell asleep with four of the choir girls snuggled in tight around me. We woke up the next morning to the amazing smell of coffee, sausage, bacon, and pancakes. What a treat! Several of the church members had come to make and serve us breakfast. We began deflating the air mattresses and ate our fabulous breakfast. We were not scheduled to do a concert at this church, but the pastor asked if we could sing a few songs for the people who had come to serve us breakfast. We headed into the sanctuary, turned on all the sound systems and got the musicians in place for a mini-concert. As usual, by the end of the performance, there was not a dry eye in the congregation. As usual, Bianca, was the most worshipful member of the choir and sang with the biggest smile on the stage.

As we were loading up the bus and van, I kept hearing people asking, "Where is Samaika?" No one seemed to know where she was. I walked around the bus, and in the middle of the parking lot, I saw Samaika, one of our choir members, leisurely walking around as if she was engaged in conversation with someone. I yelled her name trying to get her attention. She didn't acknowledge me. I kept walking toward her, calling out her name. Still with no response, I continued forward. When I reached her, she was just standing there in a daze. I took her by the hand, and she finally looked at me. I said "Samaika, why are you out here in the middle of the parking lot by yourself?" She said "I'm not by myself. I came with the little boy!" "What little boy?" I asked. She said "I don't know, he didn't tell me his name. He came inside while we were eating breakfast and asked me to come outside with him and we've been walking and talking." I started shaking my head and did my best to remain calm so she would continue talking to me. "Where is the little boy now?" I asked. She looked around the parking lot and said "I don't know, I don't see him now. Maybe he went home?" I kept holding her close to me and walked back inside the church. The pastor's wife saw us and said "Oh, I see you found Samaika!" I just smiled and said "Yes, we did."

We loaded up our final items and were finally ready to get on the road. We pulled out of the church and Magine, our youngest choir member, was staring intently at the steeple of the church. Mirlanda, another choir member, tapped me on the shoulder and said, "Mommy Linda, look at that mean, black bird on top of the steeple at the church." "Yes, I see it, Mirlanda." "That's who Samaika was talking to in the parking lot Mommy Linda. He's been here since last night when we got here." I just loaded the kids into the bus and drove off toward the highway to our next destination, wondering if there was a connection between voodoo and a raven?

WHEN I FIRST HEARD
THE NAME JEREMY

CHAPTER SIX

Isaiah 43:2

When you pass through the waters, I will be with you; and when you pass through the rivers, they will not sweep over you. When you walk through the fire, you will not be burned; the flames will not set you ablaze.

Mommy Linda with the musicians and interpreter (this picture was experiencing their first snow!)

One evening, I had the rare opportunity to have a conversation with just the musicians. None of the children from the choir were around. We were talking about many different things that had happened during the choir tour, and spoke about their future and the possibility of attending college, a dream for all the boys that I wanted to make a reality. At one point in the conversation, the topic of the three girls who were often involved in the manifestations came up. Mostly, the guys were looking for some sympathy given how late they'd had to stay up, in order to help control whichever one of the three girls was having a manifestation on any given night. They were understandably tired, and they were complaining – in a nice way -- about having to help. I apologized to them and told them how grateful I was for all their help.

One of the musicians, the biological son of Paul and Gertrude, the man and woman who ran the LifeSaver orphanage in Haiti, spoke up. Having lived with all the girls for years, he said "Mommy Linda, did you know that the three girls we are having problems with all have relatives who are very heavily involved in voodoo?" "Excuse me?" I asked. He continued, "Yes, Mommy Linda, two of them actually have an uncle who is a head voodoo priest. His name is Jeremy. We have seen him before. He is crazy! We all think that Jeremy has placed voodoo curses on those girls."

Not believing what I was hearing, I asked, "What? Are you serious? No. That doesn't even make sense. Why in the world would anyone do that?" And then, for the first time throughout all this madness, I heard the most logical explanation ever. "Because, Mommy Linda, the voodoo people are very jealous. They are jealous that we all got to come to the United States from Haiti, and they did not." He continued "They are even more upset because the reason we are here is to sing about Jesus and to share the gospel."

I was in shock but intently listening. I sat quietly digesting what this young man was saying. It certainly made sense. It was crazy, but it made sense. Thinking through every incident that had occurred, it really made me angry, but it made sense. Then he kept talking. "Some people came to the orphanage before we left for America for this year's choir tour and told us they had learned something new." Not fully understanding what he meant, I asked, "What do you mean something new?" He replied, "They said the voodoo people in Haiti now know how to astro-project, and they were very proud that they would be able to visit the children spiritually and cast spells on us while we were in the United States."

The first time I witnessed the demonic attack within Michelin, my first reaction was disbelief and fear. Not knowing what to believe, and whether or not to trust what I had seen and heard, I watched and prayed. When the first attack turned into a second, and the second turned into a third, my weary spirit was ready to call in the experts to bring it all to an end. After repeatedly being told it won't happen again, followed by yet another incident, I was desperate for answers. I was in the middle of a major spiritual battle between heaven and the demonic realm! I had my closest community fasting, praying and seeking God for help with this nightmare! I turned to scripture, absorbing every resource available to me on the spiritual realm. I was ready to brandish the sword of truth and fight in the spiritual realm through the Holy Spirit's power in me. I fought hard with prayer and truth, but as the attacks continued without reprieve, I grew tired. It became increasingly tempting to shut down the tour and just send the kids home. Members of our core Bible Study group fasted and prayed. Our Board of Directors were on 24 hour prayer vigils. We searched the Word and sought counsel. This was not just me looking for answers but many who were closely involved. Throughout our choir tour, I knew I had a daily choice I'd have to make... I could continue down the path of fear, frustration, and perceived failure, or I could fight. With the first big puzzle piece in hand, that day I was ready to fight.

Ready to jump on a plane and confront the problem head on through whatever means necessary, I asked, "Where is this voodoo priest Jeremy?" He responded, "Oh, I don't know. I've only seen him a couple of times and from a distance. Everyone is very scared of him. He is very powerful." The other musicians began chiming in because they had also heard of Jeremy. "What do I have to do to meet him?" I asked. After a pause, all of them started laughing hysterically. "Oh, Mommy Linda, that would never happen! Even if it could happen, that would be a horrible idea and we would never let you meet him, it would be too dangerous." I walked away from our conversation with a firm conviction on my mind and in my heart. Challenge accepted. Little did I know the battle had just begun!

MOTHER EMANUEL

CHAPTER SEVEN

Philippians 4:6-7

Do not be anxious about anything, but in every situation, by prayer and petition, with thanksgiving, present your requests to God. And the peace of God, which transcends all understanding, will guard your hearts and your minds in Christ Jesus.

Love Him Love Them Haitian Choir singing at Mother Emmanuel in Charleston

On the road again, we were halfway through an eight-hour drive from West Virginia to Charleston, South Carolina. I could feel the Holy Spirit prompting me as I was driving the bus toward Charleston. While calling the churches prior to arrival to confirm the choir was the responsibility of others within our ministry so it seemed strange for me to call but, I was obedient to the prompting I felt, and personally made a telephone call to the church. A female voice answered, "Mother Emmanuel AME, how may I help you?" I cheerfully responded by introducing myself, "Hi, this is Linda Gunter with the Love Him Love Them Haitian Orphan Choir." Not totally sure why I was prompted to call, I continued with our normal run through. "I just wanted to touch base with you and let you know we are on our way. I also wanted to see where the best place is going to be for us to meet up with the person who will take us to where we will be staying tonight."

There was dead silence on the phone. I assumed we had been disconnected so I pulled my cell phone out from my ear to look, but it said we were connected. So, I began again "Hello, ma'am?" I could hear a voice on the other end this time asking, "Now, who is this again?"

"It's Linda, Linda Gunter with the Love Him Love Them Haitian orphan choir. Our choir is scheduled to sing at your church service tomorrow morning?" My statement had somehow turned into a question. There was silence again, so I continued. "We were planning to stay at a dorm facility you have there at the church tonight?" Again, for some reason I was now asking it as a question instead of confirming it. Again, there was another long pause. I just kept going. "We were counting on you to feed us tonight and then to provide lunch tomorrow after church." I was gaining my confidence and switched back to a statement instead of a question, and then there was a response.

"Ma'am, everything in this town is flooded. We don't have any place for you to stay, and you won't find anywhere in town where you can stay. I don't see anything written down saying ya'll are singing at our church tomorrow. Wait, here is a note, but it just says ya'll are coming to the service, not singing at the service. We let groups come all the time, but I'm sorry, ya'll won't be staying here tonight or singing tomorrow. The dorms we have are all flooded."

While still on the phone, I took a very deep breath. I was wrestling with the fact that we still had a five-hour drive ahead of us, to reach Charleston. I needed to find dinner for 30 … and a place to stay for the night. The next morning, we would need to find breakfast for the kids, not to mention a new location to sing -- since, apparently, we were not singing at Mother Emmanuel AME. After taking a moment to compose myself, I repeated the entire scenario back to the lady on the phone again just to be sure I had understood her correctly. Then I added in my final question, "Is there anywhere you can think of that we might be able to find a place to sleep tonight?"

She asked, "How many people are in your group again?" I replied in a soft tone of voice, because I was so afraid of the response. I often received the same gasp in response, whenever I told anyone about the number of people traveling in our group, so I almost whispered "30!" Her response was very clear and loud, "Oh, Lord! No, you won't find anywhere around here for a group that size. Most everyone who lives here can't even get into their own home, because of the flood, so all of the hotel rooms in the area are booked." Now, my voice was quivering as I heard myself ask, "Is there any way we could just sing a couple of songs tomorrow at the church?" She responded, "Oh honey, I can't answer that. I have to speak with the Pastor." With a still shaking voice, I said "Would it be possible for you to call me back just to let me know what he says?" Her response was, "I'll try."

Despite the discouraging phone call, we continued our drive towards Charleston, as we were already four hours into our eight-hour drive. As I was driving the bus, I was thinking out loud, in an effort to think of every contact we had in the Charleston area. Still, finding a place for 30 people to stay, only four hours later, proved to be quite problematic. The idea of finding a place to sing the next day, in a town that most residents had evacuated three or four days earlier because of an approaching flood, was yet another challenge.

I kept driving, and after every one of my calls met with no encouraging response, I decided to call my husband David. I did my best to explain the situation. I was thinking that perhaps we could use some of his Holiday Inn points at one of their hotels that provided complimentary breakfast. I still had no idea how we would feed everyone for dinner. David said he would look online and see what he could come up with. Then I decided to pray. I prayed, "God, you are the only one who can fix this. I'm out of possible solutions. I need you to answer now, please!"

While I was waiting for David to get back to me, the lady from the Mother Emmanuel AME church called me back. She had spoken with the Pastor, who said we could come to their morning service and sing two songs. They were not able to house or feed us that evening or Sunday morning, however, and she would have to see about lunch the following day. Upon hanging up with her, my phone immediately rang, and David was on the line. "Okay, you've got four rooms booked."

I took down all the details, and then I remembered that, not long ago, someone had given us Chick-fil-A gift cards for such a time as this!

We pulled into the hotel around six o'clock, and quickly checked in. We divided up kids and chaperones into the four rooms. Directly behind the hotel was a mall that included a Chick-fil-A restaurant. We handed out the Chick- fil-A gift cards and walked to the mall in groups to eat, and then quickly called it a night.

We departed from the hotel the next morning and arrived at Mother Emmanuel AME. It was very surreal feeling, one that I don't ever remember feeling before. It was the church that 21-year-old Dylan Roof walked into on the evening of June 17, 2015 and proceeded to murder nine people, including the Senior Pastor. The tragedy became known as the Charleston Church Massacre. Of course, the children in the choir would have no way of knowing anything about this horrific incident, and I don't really think any of our interns or volunteers realized we were in the same place that this terrible tragedy occurred. Without realizing it, the room that we were assigned for our costume changes was the very same room where the shooting had occurred. We very gratefully ate donuts provided by the church – especially appreciated because the hotel where we stayed didn't have any breakfast available. The church secretary told us that the choir needed to quickly change into their performance costumes. She explained that we would need to sit through the entire service, both before and after we sang. It was very seldom, if ever, that was required. We were always responsible for the entire service everywhere we sang. We were almost always on stage, where we could be VERY loud and high energy – and the members of our choir didn't have any experience sitting anywhere quietly for any length of time. As you can imagine, it can be a challenge to keep 30 children, ages 4 – 18, still, let alone quiet, anywhere or for anything. I had no idea how we would handle this request from the church leaders. Then, miraculously, out of nowhere, an entire team of people showed up to surprise us! That morning, they had driven 200 miles to Charleston from Charlotte, North Carolina. Many members of this large group were college students, and some had brought friends and family with them. Most of our surprise guests had previously joined us on mission trips to Haiti, where they first met the kids with a visit to LifeSaver orphanage. They were very excited to have this chance to see the children perform in America. This large group of college students and their friends helped us by sitting amongst the kids to help monitor their behavior.

Thankfully, the children sat very respectfully and attentively in this conservative, quiet sanctuary during what was probably, at minimum, going to be a 60-minute sermon in a language they didn't understand. What a blessing!

We did our best to follow the program in the bulletin we had each been handed upon arrival. At the nod of the music director, I stood to give an abbreviated version of our story while the choir was making their way to the front of the church and the musicians were headed to their instruments. We sang two songs. As usual, there was not a dry eye in the congregation. We returned to our assigned seats, which happened to be located in the front three rows of the church. Bianca, one of the older girls in the choir, had somehow managed to make it all the way to the back of the church and ended up sitting with our friends Sarah Logan and her mom Becky, who were members of the group who drove from Charlotte to surprise us.

The church's new pastor, Eric Manning, took the stage after the choir's performance and preached an amazing sermon on the family. He alluded to an event involving his son that had happened the previous week, and how God was working in his own family. He gave an altar call and asked for any parents in the room who had a wayward child to come to the altar. The altar filled up very quickly with parents praying. I happened to be standing right beside Pastor Manning's wife, and we were praying for each other.

A few moments into the altar call I felt a tug on my skirt. I ignored it at first, but the tugging was persistent. I looked down and it was Magine. She was pointing to the right side of the altar and saying "Look, look Mommy Linda, Bianca is sick." Again, "sick" had become our codeword. Magine wasn't letting me know about a physical illness, but rather a spiritual attack. I was on the far-left side of the church and had to work my way through the large group of people at the altar, to reach Bianca. Once I had moved to a spot next to Bianca, there were already three or four people on the ground, hovering over her. To the untrained eye, it appeared as though Bianca was having a full-blown seizure. However, to those of us who knew Bianca, we knew it was a demonic manifestation.

Pastor Manning made his way down from the pulpit to see the source of this ruckus. Several people had already called 911, and we could hear the sirens of the approaching ambulances. I was on my knees on the floor, hovering over Bianca with Pastor Manning right beside me. As we both were praying, I looked over to him and said, "You do realize this is not a medical problem, right?" His eyes locked with mine and he said very quietly, "Yes, I do." We both laid our hands on Bianca and continued to pray very quietly. There was a lady from the congregation who was at Bianca's feet, and she was screaming out her prayers. As we continued praying and just before the paramedics made it to the front of the church, Bianca was "back." The demon who had taken over her body left, mere seconds before the paramedics arrived to measure her vital signs. As the paramedics were asking me questions and placing Bianca on a stretcher to roll her out of the church, Pastor Manning climbed back up into the pulpit and addressed the congregation. Most were in shock because of what they had just witnessed. He said, "Satan does not like the family. I have been trying to explain spiritual warfare to you, but to no avail. Now, you just got to experience it firsthand."

Bianca was rolled through to the vestibule of the church, where I was attempting to speak kindly, yet sternly, to the paramedics, trying to persuade them that's there was no need to take Bianca to the hospital. I assured them, "All of her vitals are normal, she is conscious and there is no sign of anything medically wrong." Frustrated with my inability to persuade them there was really nothing medically wrong with Bianca, I was on the verge of unraveling. One of the paramedics placed her hands on my arm and kindly said, "It's okay, we understand. We just need you to sign this paperwork stating that you're refusing medical transport to the hospital." I signed the paperwork and they left.

By the time the paramedics left, our surprise visitors from Charlotte, our volunteers and our choir mom, Alana, had taken the other children back downstairs to their changing room, where they began eating lunch. I realized, in all the drama, the diamond from my wedding ring was missing. I made my way back to the front of the church where I had been sitting and started crawling around on the floor where I had prayed over Bianca. While I was on the floor, the pastor and his wife came back into the sanctuary. I apologized profusely for interrupting the service in such an unusual way. They both assured me there was no apology needed. Tears were flowing down my face as I formed my question. "How in the world does a demon have the nerve to show up in the middle of a church service?" His wife took my arm and said "Honey, Satan himself walked in this church two years ago and killed nine of our staff members." They both shared stories with me until the kids began trickling upstairs to get me.

I left that church that day without the diamond in my ring, and feeling more exhausted from the previous 24 hours than I'd ever felt in my life. Sarah Logan, our friend from Charlotte who sat next to Bianca during the service, later told me that she thought it was the most amazing service she had ever attended. I thought that day would of scared away any and all of those college students but instead it created a bond with them that was unbreakable. Sarah went on to be one of our interns in Haiti and all of those students came to Haiti and are still heavily involved in our ministry.

PHONE CALL

CHAPTER EIGHT

1 Peter 4:12-13

Beloved, do not be surprised at the fiery trial when it comes upon you to test you, as though something strange were happening to you. But rejoice insofar as you share Christ's sufferings, that you may also rejoice and be glad when his glory is revealed.

While much of our choir tour was spent on the road, we were thankful for a place to return to that we could call home. The choir house, where all the children ate, played and slept on the evenings we were not on the road, was provided by a dear friend, Sarah LeCroy. The house was located on the property of her private Christian school, The Barnes Academy. The school was located in Hartwell, Georgia, approximately 45 minutes away from my home. At least two to three times a week, during the first and second years of the choir tours, we would receive a phone call, usually around midnight or later from one of the volunteers staying at the house, to tell us one of three girls had just begun having a demonic manifestation. I'm not sure how it happened, but every time those calls came in, my husband David, who traveled very often with his job, was always home. He would jump out of bed and would call two or three other men to meet him at the choir house, to go and fight with one or more demons.

One of the girls was a "runner." She heard voices telling her we were trying to hurt her, and she needed to run as fast as she could to get as far away from us as possible. Another of the girls was a "thrasher." She would kick and hit and bite and bang her head against a wall or the floor. The third girl was a "strangler," and would put her hands around her own neck, squeezing harder than you can even imagine. We finally smartened up and made her cut her nails to avoid her scratching up her own face and neck, along with everyone else's exposed skin should they be within scratching distance. When any one of these three, usually sweet and polite, girls experienced a demonic manifestation, it took three to five adult men to contain and control the unbelievable strength the girls exhibited. Whether it was to keep them from running outside into the middle of a busy road (running with Olympic speed), to hold different body parts to keep oneself from being thrown up against a wall, or holding hands away to prevent a girl from strangling herself, fending off the demonic attacks required tremendous strength on all levels… spiritual, mental, and physical. All of this would go on for hours, many nights until 3 or 4 am. With all the adults in the choir house focused on these manifestations and their strenuous efforts to keep these girls alive, all the other children ran amuck. Everyone was perpetually exhausted for days, following these manifestations.

In the beginning, we kept quiet about these extraordinary incidents -- mostly because it caused anyone we told to look at us, as if we were from another planet. Anyone we did dare to tell also never seemed to come around again. We were very particular about who we told about these strange incidents. In an effort to cover all of our bases, we had all the girls tested for epilepsy and seizures, and spoke with neurologists. Every time we described what was happening to a medical professional, they just turned their heads sideways, stared at us, and ceased asking any more questions. Any and all medical tests that were run on these girls always came back negative or inconclusive. The bottom line was that the medical profession could not help us. (This experience, by the way, has given me a new understanding of why many people are locked up in mental institutions.) Knowing the medical establishment could not help us, we realized we had to look elsewhere for answers. As a result, we began to explore whether anyone we knew had any ideas regarding how to deal with demonic manifestations.

I received a text one day, telling me about several people who had experience casting out demons. To top it off, they spoke FRENCH! WOW! What more could we ask for? Creole is the official language in Haiti, but the children learn French in school. When I learned these people were willing to meet with us, I just knew our troubles were over. I loaded the three girls up in my personal vehicle instead of the bus, and we headed to their church to meet.

Upon arrival, the four of us went into the church office, where the people were waiting with their Bibles. No one seemed to know what to say. I realized after the awkward introductions, that I had previously met one of the ladies in the room. They asked the girls a few questions, all of which were met with very short answers. I suggested that it might be helpful if I provided a little background. As the team was listening very intently, as I shared what had been happening, providing graphic details of the episodes we were experiencing. After an extensive explanation, they began speaking in French to the three Haitian girls. I studied French in high school, but I was not able to follow the conversation. My head kept bobbing back and forth, trying to keep up. I realized after a few moments that one of the team members was presenting the plan of salvation. I interrupted and said, "They have all already asked Jesus to be their Lord and Savior." They continued with their presentation in French and had each girl repeat a prayer. They handed the girls some gospel tracts written in French, and as we were walking back out to the parking lot, they told me, "Don't worry, it will never happen again."

THE HOLY SPIRIT

CHAPTER NINE

Acts 2:1-4

When the day of Pentecost came, they were all together in one place. Suddenly a sound like the blowing of a violent wind came from heaven and filled the whole house where they were sitting. They saw what seemed to be tongues of fire that separated and came to rest on each of them. All of them were filled with the Holy Spirit and began to speak in other tongues as the Spirit enabled them.

By this time, we had already taken the girls to more places than I could count, trying to find someone who could take care of our "problem." Each time, I had been told, "Don't worry, this will never happen again." I finally felt like I had no other option, and I decided to take matters into my own hands. Instead of reaching out to other people who had "experience," I started reading everything I could find about demons. I memorized Psalms 91. I started reading the Bible, day and night and seeking God's help. As I began searching through the Bible to find information on demons, I was overwhelmed. I could not believe how many stories were in the Bible, my Bible, the Bible I had always read, about demons. Driven by my quest to learn more about demons, it was as if I had never read the Bible before, which was far from the truth. It seemed like every page I turned, that's all Jesus dealt with. He was either healing somebody, raising someone from the dead or casting out a demon. I thought back to when I used to wear a W.W.J.D. (What Would Jesus Do?) bracelet. No one ever told me or even talked about casting out demons. And yet, according to the Bible, the Word of God, that was a part of Jesus' ministry.

Then I read about Jesus saying that after He left this earth, He would send the Holy Spirit. Those of us who believe would then have the power to do even greater things than what Jesus had done. What?! I read there was a baptism of the Holy Spirit and fire. This event was supposed to be completely separate from salvation. I learned that I could have a prayer language that would allow the Holy Spirit to speak and pray for me in situations when I didn't know how or what to pray. At one point when I was reading my Bible, I truly thought someone had inexplicably switched out the words in my Bible. I started using five different translations and would lay them all out on my desk at the same time to be sure I wasn't misreading something. I read in 1 John that our purpose on this earth is to demolish the works of the devil. I referenced a search engine to try to understand more, but that only confused me. I got to a point where I only read the Bible and if I felt like I needed an explanation or a commentary to explain something, I would just ask the Holy Spirit to personally explain it to me. Did you know there is a verse in Mark that says if you believe, you can lay your hands on the sick and they will be healed? That made me so mad! I had put my hands on those girls so many times, but they were not healed.

I began spending hours in my home office behind closed doors, searching, seeking, begging God, and praying. I concluded that if the Bible said something was supposed to happen, and it wasn't happening, then something was wrong with me.

I didn't know anyone to talk to about the baptism of the Holy Spirit or speaking in tongues. First, I had never even heard of the Baptism thing, and second, anyone I knew that "spoke in tongues" was weird. I continued my search, and tried to find intelligent experts who spoke about these topics – but most of them were extraordinarily strange. Also, all of these so-called experts seemed to be men. I couldn't find any ladies. Finally, I found a female expert by the name of Marilyn Hickey, a Christian minister based in Texas. I started listening to her recordings, and she made sense. In addition, Minister Hickey was very stylish. Her clothes and shoes always matched, and she was always well accessorized, which, if you know me, is a must! I finally felt that all my dedicated research was finally leading in a promising direction. I needed to be baptized in the Holy Spirit. I called Pastor Maxeau in Haiti one Sunday night after Bible study at our home.

I met Pastor Maxeau on our first trip to Haiti during Christmas 2011. Our friend Donald Lyons, who owned the guest house in Haiti where our family stayed on that visit – a wonderful place he named My Father's Guest House -- introduced us to him. Pastor Maxeau introduced us to two of the orphanages that our ministry supports today, the first being our choir orphanage. The second girls-only orphanage he brought us to is one we've since taken over and transformed into a new home with vocational training and new employment opportunities. Both of these orphanages are now thriving. Almost immediately, we recognized Pastor Maxeau's strength of character, his boundless vision and hope for his community, and his fire for Christ. Since first meeting him during our 2011 Christmas trip to Haiti, Pastor Maxeau has become a trusted advisor, dedicated prayer partner, fellow visionary, and most importantly, pillar of Biblical truth whenever I need a sounding board.

As soon as Maxeau picked up the phone that Sunday night, I blurted out "Have you ever been baptized in the Holy Spirit Fire?" "Of course, I have, Linda," he answered immediately. He told me the whole story. I asked him to pray for the same thing to happen to me -- and he did. As I spoke with my friend in Haiti, I was sitting on our red couch in the basement of our home in Georgia, more than one thousand miles away from one another. I put my phone on "speaker mode," and laid it in my lap. I listened as Pastor Maxeau prayed for me in a language I couldn't understand. I have continually asked God to fill me with the Holy Spirit since then. I actually feel as if the Holy Spirit "leaks out of me onto others," and I need a continual filling up!

I started praying for people the very next day. One of the first people I prayed for was a friend who had been diagnosed with Stage 4 Breast Cancer. I prayed for her, as I sat in one of the rocking chairs outside of a Cracker Barrel restaurant near my home. Two days later, she called me and said the doctor had told her the cancer was gone. I prayed for another friend who had an abscessed tooth with a swollen mouth. I prayed for her over the phone, and while I was praying, the swelling and her temperature went down, and the pain went away.

I prayed for another friend who had a heart rate that was sky high. She had been to the doctor and tried to get it under control for the past few weeks through medication, but to no avail. I could feel her heart racing when I placed my hands on her. Her heart seemed to be beating a million miles a minute.

After praying for less than 30 seconds, God returned her heartbeat to normal. I could actually feel my friend's heartbeat slowing down, as I was praying.

All this was -- and still is -- crazy to me. I could fill up the rest of this book with dozens of stories like this. I couldn't believe I had lived my entire Christian life not knowing anything about this. Furthermore, how could I have done so many Bible studies and NEVER seen any of this in the BIBLE?

SEYMA / DRIVE HOME FROM GAINESVILLE

CHAPTER TEN

Mark 16:17

And these signs will accompany those who believe: In my name
they will drive out demons; they will speak in new tongues

Late one night, as we were finally on our way home from Harmony Church in Dawsonville, Georgia, I had an experience that will be vividly etched in my mind for the rest of my life. The bus was dark and very quiet. Everyone was sleeping. Suddenly, I heard a loud ruckus in the back of the bus. I turned on all the lights, looked into the makeshift rearview mirror -- a key purchase from the local "Dollar Tree" store, mounted so I could see what was happening behind me, as I drove the bus. I could see kids jumping out of their seats, one at a time -- and then I was able to identify the source of this commotion. You may find this hard to believe, but Bianca was literally *levitating* in the air -- above the seats! It was an unbelievable sight, but one that was real, nonetheless. She was unconscious and her eyes were rolled back in her head. I yelled back from the driver's seat, "Pray!" There were already three people trying to hold her down. Now, truly in "a state of shock," I continued driving the bus, for what felt like 45 minutes -- but, in actuality, was only five minutes, so that I could find a place to pull over and park. The commotion in the back of the bus was escalating. I jumped out from behind the steering wheel, and crawled over the first seat to navigate around the kids crowding the aisle. My sole focus was to get to Bianca. I put my hands on her and commanded the demon that had obviously taken over her body to "Get out and leave!" Apparently without even realizing it, I was pointing to a graveyard that was on the other side of the parking lot. I was telling the demon to leave, and offering it a nice graveyard to go to. As I was praying, I felt this tugging on the back of my shirt accompanied with sounds of "Mommy Linda, Mommy Linda." I remember thinking, you have got to be kidding me, can't you see I am casting out a demon? At first, I ignored the tugging and the cry of my name. I kept praying and commanding the demon to leave. But the tugging on my shirt and the cries of my name continued. Finally, I turned around to see seven-year-old Seyma, a choir member, behind me. I turned to see what she wanted. She looked intently in my eyes with a very confused look and said, "Mommy Linda, you keep telling the demon to leave, but you forgot to open the bus door so the demon can go where you are telling it to go." I stopped and just stared at her. I couldn't decide if I wanted to spank her for interrupting me, yell at her for continuously saying my name, or completely ignore her and act like I didn't hear anything she said. However, after focusing on her face in the dim lights of the bus, I realized she was genuinely serious. While thinking all of this, I had yet to respond to her. Seyma said again, "Mommy Linda, open the door so the demon can go!" I turned around, walked the few feet toward the front of the bus and pushed the button to open the side door of the bus. I walked back to Bianca and yelled, "Get out!" Bianca sat up, somehow back to her normal self – and seemed to have no idea why of what was happening or why we had stopped in the parking lot.

Seyma looked over at me with a very satisfied look on her face and said, "Good job, Mommy Linda! Let's go, now. And next time, Mommy Linda, don't forget to open the door!" I responded, "Don't worry Seyma, it will never happen again!"

We have passed that same church parking lot on many occasions every time we drive through Gainesville, Georgia. Every time, someone says, "Remember when Mommy Linda forgot to open the door?"

Mommy Linda and precious Seyma

GSHAC

CHAPTER ELEVEN

1 Peter 5:8-11

Be alert and of sober mind. Your enemy the devil prowls around like a roaring lion looking for someone to devour. Resist him, standing firm in the faith, because you know that the family of believers throughout the world is undergoing the same kind of sufferings. And the God of all grace, who called you to his eternal glory in Christ, after you have suffered a little while, will himself restore you and make you strong, firm and steadfast. To him be the power for ever and ever. Amen.

The night before the last night of the 2017 choir tour, we sang at a Haitian church in Lawrenceville, Georgia. They made us a fabulous Haitian meal and it was an amazing concert. Because 90% of the congregation was Haitian, I felt at liberty to share openly and candidly about the ongoing demonic manifestations and spiritual warfare we had been experiencing for the past two years. I also shared about all the amazing accomplishments that God was doing in Haiti, through the choir. The pastor closed out the concert by challenging the congregation, stating that Love Him Love Them was doing in Haiti what the church should be doing.

At the end of the concert, we were flooded with people at the product table – where we offered jewelry, books and other items for sale, with the proceeds supporting the work of our ministry. Everyone had so many questions. As the crowd started to thin out, we began packing up the instruments and items from the product table. Magine came over, and began tugging on my shirt. She said, "Mommy Linda, Bianca is sick on the bus." I turned to run out the door of the church and saw the pastor and two other men from his staff. As I was running out the door, I literally yelled out, "If you want to see what I was talking about tonight, it's happening on the bus outside. One of the girls is having a demonic manifestation right now." All three came running out behind me.

As we approached the bus, we could see that my husband David was holding Bianca's feet, and two of our musicians were trying to hold her hands. She was stretched across the aisle of the bus. The three pastors got on the bus, and took the place of David and our two musicians. We rarely had anyone come to our aid like this. As they stepped aside, David and the musicians kept a close eye on what was happening. The three pastors prayed in the Creole language for 15 minutes. The rest of the choir remained outside, running around in the parking lot, just outside the bus playing. This experience was so common to them it didn't even faze them.

After praying, the pastors walked off the bus and said "Ok, she's fine. Don't worry, it will never happen again!" As Bianca was walking off the bus after the pastors, saying she needed to use the bathroom, my husband David caught her eyes from the lights from the parking lot. He immediately said, "NO, that's not Bianca!" He reached out to grab her arm and she slipped right through his fingers. He yelled "Stop her!" She ran with the speed of a bolt of lightning heading straight for the busy street in front of the church. Every child and adult in the parking lot was running after her. Those of us who were not fast enough stood back at the end of the bus and gasped as we watched Bianca run directly *through* a vehicle, the driver never even seeming to have noticed her, neither stopping nor braking. Every other vehicle on the road slammed on their brakes to avoid hitting the other children and adults who ran out into the road after Bianca.

Finally, one of our musicians caught up to and grabbed Bianca -- and with the help of four others, they struggled to constrain her brute strength, and carried her back to the church. They took her into the pastor's office, and by the time they laid her on the floor in the office, she had turned back into our sweet, loving Bianca. She had no idea what had happened. As two pastors sat and spoke with Bianca in Creole, I sat with the Senior Pastor and broke down into a fit of sobbing. All I could think was that in a matter of 10 seconds, we almost lost 20 of our 30 children, as they chased after Bianca into the midst of a busy stream of traffic – all because they hoped to save her life.

I cried out, "This is it! I'm finished! I quit! I give up! I just want to get these kids back to Haiti! And I can't wait to find the relatives who placed these voodoo curses on them. I'm done. And the relatives are going to be done when I find them." The pastor grabbed me by the shoulders and said, "Stop it! Stop it!" He exclaimed, "Don't you realize you are fighting Satan head on? You cannot continue to present the gospel to crowds of people two times a day and not expect warfare! You are NOT going to quit!"

I was too overwhelmed, too crushed by what I had just seen, to really hear him. I yelled back, "Yes I am! I'm finished! This is ridiculous! All of our children almost died tonight; it's not worth it!" He still had his hands on my shoulders, and now he started shaking me. "Mommy Linda, do you not realize you just witnessed a MIRACLE tonight? That child ran through a car, and 20 other children ran into oncoming traffic and not one of them was injured. You are not quitting."

The same three pastors that had prayed for Bianca prayed for me.

I left that church and drove the 90 minutes back to the choir house -- mad, exhausted and thinking, "Don't worry, this choir tour will never happen again."

OUR LAST NIGHT IN AMERICA IN 2017 AND THE TRIP HOME TO HAITI THE NEXT DAY

CHAPTER TWELVE

Mark 11:25

And when you stand praying, if you hold anything against anyone, forgive them, so that your Father in heaven may forgive you your sins.

Love Him Love Them Haitian Choir singing at Mercedes Benz stadium in Atlanta Georgia

Our last night in America in 2017 was an amazing opportunity, and after the previous evening at the Haitian church, with all its drama, it was a welcome event! We sang the national anthem at the opening game for the Atlanta United soccer team in the brand-new Mercedes Benz stadium in Atlanta. They treated us like royalty. We condensed our story about the children coming to America to 45 seconds, and the announcer quickly shared about the orphans who had lost their families in the 2010 earthquake. The crowd roared with applause when we finished singing the national anthem. We stayed for the game. The children, and even the musicians, who were often very difficult to impress, had an amazing time watching the soccer game. Soccer -- or football, as they referred to it in Haiti -- is their favorite sport. We stayed in a hotel in Atlanta that night, close to the airport, in preparation for our flight to Haiti the next day.

We headed to the airport early the next morning and made our flight without any problems. We left the musicians and our interpreter behind in the U.S., so they could each begin to pursue their dream of a college education. As a result, I was the only adult flying to Haiti with the kids. At this point in the tour, that really wasn't as big of a deal as it may sound. It was the children's fourth time on a plane, and their English had improved tremendously, since that first trip to the U.S. Once everyone was settled, I took my seat on the plane, put my seat back in a recline position, and closed my eyes. My thoughts went immediately to a vivid video playing in my mind of all the horrible things that had occurred over the past two years with Bianca, Samaika and Micheline. I remembered my conversation with the musicians, as they told me about the girls' Uncle Jeremy, and his involvement in voodoo. I decided at that moment on the plane that I was going to set up a meeting with this voodoo priest when I got to Haiti. To be brutally honest, my initial thoughts were centered around the idea of killing him. I wanted to hurt him, punish him, and yell at him. I really wanted to find some way to hurt him for all the trouble, fiascos, grief, sleepless nights and pain he had caused me, many other people, and especially the girls. My only problem was I couldn't figure out how I was going to find him in Haiti. At that very moment, I heard God speak very clearly to me. "Linda, you will find Jeremy and you will meet with him, but you are not going to kill him. You are going to lead him to me." I spoke out loud "No, I am not!" When I realized I was speaking out loud I opened my eyes. I said again under my breath, "Lord, there is no way I'm telling him about you. I only want to hurt him the same way he has hurt us for the past two years."

Apparently, the conversation was over, because I didn't hear anything else. I slept the rest of the flight. We landed safely in Haiti. I parted ways with the children at the airport, but not before making arrangements to go to the beach the next day for a big celebration. I went to spend the night at the guesthouse, and the children all returned to the orphanage.

The next morning, I arrived at the orphanage in the huge cattle truck, which was the only transportation we had that could hold all of us. We were prepared for a wonderful day at the beautiful beach in Haiti. As all of the children were piling into the truck, I pulled Paul William, the director of the orphanage, to the side and told him I wanted him to contact the girls' Uncle Jeremy and have him meet me at the orphanage when I returned from the beach with the kids later that night. His eyes almost popped out of his head. He asked, "Jeremy? Jeremy, who?" I said, "Jeremy, the voodoo priest." Startled, he looked at me as if I was a ghost and said, "How do you know about Jeremy?" I explained to him, "Your sons told me the whole story. I want to meet him." Paul responded, "There is no way for me to contact him, Mommy Linda, and even if I could find him, he cannot come to the orphanage. He is a very dangerous and a very powerful, evil man. I cannot help you with this request." I looked back at Paul William as seriously and as intently as I knew how and said, "He needs to be here when we return from the beach today." Many of the nosy and curious children overheard my conversation.

I jumped up into the cattle truck with all the kids to leave. We were headed to the Wahoo Bay Beach Club and Resort, north of Port-au-Prince, for the day. Situated on a beautiful spot on the ocean, and nestled between majestic mountains, the resort also features a swimming pool.

Pastor Maxeau was with us for the trip, so while he was at the pool watching some kids, I was at the beach with the other children. After swimming, we all enjoyed a great lunch at the resort. It was a fabulous day in the Caribbean and an incredible blessing for the kids, considering most Haitians, though born on an island nation, never in their lifetime get to see the ocean. On the two-hour drive back to the orphanage, we got stuck in traffic because of protestors in the streets. At one point in our trip, we just sat in the middle of the road without moving for over 90 minutes. After what totaled a 5-hour drive, we finally pulled back into the orphanage. I was exhausted and ready for the kids to get off the truck so we could continue to drive the additional 90 minutes to the guest house for a cold shower and then bed. As we pulled into the orphanage, I started hearing, "Look Mommy Linda, the voodoo people are here." I didn't really pay attention at first. Now all of the children were saying and almost singing, "Mommy Linda, the voodoo people are here." I was focused on making sure everyone was getting their belongings off the truck.

It had been a long day and all the kids were finally ready to run inside and go straight to bed. I went inside the orphanage to tuck the children in and say good night. Paul William met me at the bottom of the steps. "O.K. Mommy Linda, I did the best I could to meet your request. Jeremy's daughter is here." I was so tired, I started to form the words on my lips to ask who Jeremy was and why was his daughter here. All at once the pieces of the puzzle came together in my mind. I had completely forgotten my demand that morning to have the voodoo priest Jeremy at the orphanage upon our return from the beach. Paul William waved his hands directing me to go up the stairs to where the voodoo people were.

As I began walking up the stairs, Pastor Maxeau came into the orphanage from the cattle truck to get me. He wanted to know what was stalling me. He reminded me we still had another 90-minute drive, and that it was not a good idea for a "blanco" (a white person) to be out on the streets in Haiti after dark. I motioned for him to follow me up the steps. During the trip up the 15 steps, I explained to Maxeau my plan to kill, hurt and punish the people who had caused all the struggles we had on the choir tours with the girls. He followed me, listening intently. Arriving at the top of the stairs, I looked to my right and saw what looked like a 20-year-old lady and a young man in his early 30's. They looked like Haitian Ken and Barbie dolls. He was very clean cut and handsome, and she was absolutely gorgeous. Paul

William introduced us to this young couple, and he brought chairs for us to sit and talk. The generator was running, so we could have light. I sat down and stared at both of them. They did not look like voodoo people to me. I had no idea what voodoo people looked like, but I didn't think they should look as perfect as this handsome young couple.

Paul William spoke in Creole, and Pastor Maxeau translated for me. The gorgeous lady was Lisa, Jeremy's daughter. She was also Samika's mother and Bianca's sister. The gentleman was Lisa's boyfriend, and his name was Kenol. At this point in my life, I knew enough Creole to get a point across. However, my mind was so boggled by what I just heard, there was no way I could even put a sentence together. Thankfully, Pastor Maxeau could interpret for all of us, even though I am certain he probably filtered my conversation and made everything sound nicer than the way I intended. However, much of communication is non-verbal, so I knew they understood the absolute disgust and confusion that I expressed through my facial expressions, even if Pastor Maxeau did not tell them what I said, word for word.

As I was asking for everything to be explained, Bianca and Samaika came into the room where we were sitting and gave Lisa the traditional Haitian greeting of kisses on the cheek. Seeing this as confirmation of what I had previously heard, I glanced at Maxeau, who looked at me and nodded as if to say, yes, you understood the situation correctly. I waited for the kids to leave, and then spoke out loud as if I were solving a math problem.

"So, YOU are Bianca's sister?"

Lisa nodded yes.

"And YOU are also Samaika's mother?" "Wi", she responded.

I hung my head. I kept saying under my breath, "I don't understand." Then I looked up and said, "So that means that Bianca is Samaika's aunt?" Everyone in the room nodded their heads, yes.

"So why in the world are those kids living in this orphanage?" Pastor Maxeau didn't even interpret my question for them to have an opportunity to respond. He just answered for them and said, "Because their elders can't take care of them." Why not?" I blurted out. "They look fine to me!" Again, Pastor Maxeau did his best to bring my anger down a notch or two, and then interpreted their responses. He said, "They both live with Lisa's mom." I tried to comprehend what this meant, and I said, "You live with your mom?" She said "Yes." "And is that Bianca's mom also?" She understood that question and said, "Yes."

Pastor Maxeau looked at me and said, "Calm down, Linda." I took a breath and then said, "I do not understand. If you and your boyfriend can live with your mother, why can't your daughter and your sister live with you?" Pastor Maxeau seemed to interpret what I said. They both responded in unison, "Because there is no room and there is no food and we do not have any money to send them to school."

I changed the subject and said, "Do you have any idea what has been happening to these girls?" They looked very confused. I began giving them graphic details of some of the worst nights I could remember us experiencing over the past two years. I told the stories at lightning bolt speed, and never once slowed down or paused long enough for Pastor Maxeau to interpret. He already knew all the stories, so he kept up with me, word for word. I think I passionately rattled off the details for a full two minutes, without taking a breath. Then, as I described Samaika beating her head up against the wall and the floor for hours, I saw a tear roll down Lisa's face. It didn't even faze me. I kept going. I had two years' worth of stories, and I could go on all night long.

Lisa's boyfriend Kenol put his hands up in the air and interrupted. Maxeau interpreted, "Something must have gone wrong." "What?" I asked. "What do you mean something must have gone wrong?" Lisa responded, "When the girls were very young, they were both very sick. My father Jeremy did something to help them. It sounds like maybe something went wrong." I yelled, "Ya' think?" Pastor Maxeau did not interpret that. I sat on the edge of my chair, staring into the eyes of both of them. I asked, "What exactly do you mean, your father 'did something?'" Lisa's one tear had now turned into many more. Kenol responded for her. "Paul William told us you know that Jeremy is a voodoo priest. Now you know he put a spell on the girls, so they would not be sick. Something has gone wrong with that spell, and we need to fix it." "We?" I asked Kenol. Kenol put his head down while he explained that he was one of Jeremy's assistants with the voodoo. He told me they could go and sacrifice a pig tonight in a ceremony and it would resolve the whole situation.

At this point, I felt like I was in a movie scene and just didn't see the cameras. I responded back to Kenol, "YOU? You do voodoo?" He kept his head down and nodded his head, yes. He got up and started to walk toward the stairs to leave, and I said, "No! Wait! Stop!" He was standing by the stairs and said, "I know exactly what needs to happen, I can go now and have the problem solved by midnight." I could see Lisa out of the corner of my eye -- still crying, but shaking her head yes in agreement, that Kenol and her father Jeremy could resolve the problems we had been suffering with for over two years in less than two hours.

I was so mad and frustrated and could not believe what I was hearing. I looked back at Lisa, and asked her how she could be so sure this solution Kenol was describing would work. She hung her head and said, "I know because I am a voodoo princess." Oh, my goodness, the children were right, the voodoo people were here! Pastor Maxeau just looked at me. I have no idea where the next words that came out of my mouth originated.

I said, "Kenol, Lisa... Do you know who Jesus Christ is?" Before I knew it, I was presenting the plan of salvation to these two voodoo people that I hated. The more I kept talking to them about Jesus and the plan he had for their lives, the less I hated them and by the time we were finished, I loved them. Both of them were crying by the end and stripping off voodoo items they had hidden under their clothes. They kept the items with them, at all times, for both protection and to use for spells and curses. They handed me red silk scarves, cross necklaces, and voodoo trinkets. As they took the items off and handed them to me, Paul William came and took them from me and burned every item in a fire just a few steps away from us. They both wanted to fully give and commit their lives to Jesus. Then Kenol stopped and said, "I need to wait until tomorrow to make my full commitment to Jesus because I need to go and help Jeremy sacrifice the pig tonight, to release the spell on the girls." I yelled out "NO! we are not going to do it that way. Today is the day of salvation! If you want to call Jeremy and have him do a silly spell, you can, but you are not doing voodoo spells anymore. Never again, from this moment forward." With that, a huge smile of freedom came over both of their faces, and they bowed their heads and prayed their own prayers of repentance and asked God to forgive them. They renounced voodoo and asked God to help them with their faith and to make Jesus the Lord of their life. When Lisa said "Amen," and raised her head, she looked at me and said, "I have so much more voodoo paraphernalia at my house, can I please bring it here to you tomorrow?" I looked at Maxeau and he nodded yes. We agreed to meet back at the orphanage the next day. We hugged as if we had been friends for years.

As Maxeau and I made the 90-minute drive home that evening, I had a million questions. But my biggest question was, would they really come back to the orphanage the next day to meet us?

Some of the items they handed over to me
Kenol and Lisa used in their voodoo ceremonies

THE NEXT DAY / WOULD THEY REALLY COME BACK?

CHAPTER THIRTEEN

Matthew 16:22 (The Voice)

The eye is the lamp of the body. You draw light into your body through your eyes, and light shines out to the world through your eyes. So if your eye is well and shows you what is true, then your whole body will be filled with light.

Pastor Maxeau and I arrived at the orphanage the next day, as previously arranged with Kenol and Lisa. They were already there, waiting for us. Lisa carried a simple plastic bag, a broken drawstring holding it together.

As soon as she saw me coming, she started opening the bag. It was obvious she wanted to get rid of everything she had in the bag as quickly as possible. She pulled out a baby blue dress and an 8 1/2" x 11" framed photo of her in the blue dress. She described it as her princess dress. The picture of her in the dress was obviously from some type of formal Voodoo ceremony. With everything she took from the bag, we followed the same process we had from the evening before. We burned everything. As beautiful as they both looked the night before, they both had a new look today, a fresh look. They had a light in their eyes. It is true that your eyes are the window to your soul. We all sat down together again, and most importantly, I wanted to confirm that Kenol had not gone to see Jeremy the night before. Kenol began with so much excitement in his voice. "Oh, Mommy Linda, I did go to see Jeremy last night." He paused for Pastor Maxeau to interpret for me. He continued. "I told him everything. I told him Lisa and I both gave our lives to Jesus Christ, and I told him about the girls. Mommy Linda, God sent you here. I have just been waiting for you to come and tell us about Jesus. It's like God told you everything we needed to hear. Thank you! Thank you! Thank you!"

Lisa in her voodoo princess dress she wore for ceremonies

Lisa handing over to Mommy Linda her Blue voodoo princess dress and other items she used in voodoo ceremonies

Burning the items they handed over

Kenol, Lisa, Mommy Linda and Pastor Maxeau after they had surrendered their lives to the Lord and given up all of their voodoo garb. Notice the Love Him Love Them bracelets on everyone's arms.)

Tears were uncontrollably rolling down my face. I didn't think this would be a good time for me to tell him my original plan to reign down destruction on everyone who had a part in the manifestations experienced by the girls. Instead, I said "Okay, Kenol, we have three more steps we need to take care of. First, do you both have a Bible?" They both answered "Yes." I thought that was strange. "Second," I continued, "we need to plan for both of you to be baptized." They were both very excited about this. Then I said, "Lastly, you have to either get married or one of you has to move out. You cannot live together if you are not married. So, what do you want to do?" Without pause they both said they really, really wanted to get married. I said "Great, then that's the answer!"

Before they could say anything further, Maxeau responded, "Linda, they can't afford to get married. They don't have any way to do that." Before I knew it, I said "Okay, here is the deal I have for you. I will pay for your wedding and provide everything you need for the wedding. You can have the ceremony here at the orphanage. The choir will sing." Their eyes grew even brighter. I pulled out my calendar to choose a date for the wedding. I wanted it to coincide with our Christmas Mission trip so we would already be in Haiti. We chose the date. They agreed it all sounded perfect. I said, "I only have one condition on this agreement. They were both staring at Maxeau waiting for him to interpret the condition. "You have to bring Jeremy here to the orphanage to meet with me the day before the wedding, okay?" They looked at each other and then agreed they could do that. I reiterated that if I did not meet with Jeremy the day before the wedding, the whole deal would be off. They both said they understood.

I left that afternoon and flew back to the United States.

MEETING THE FATHER OF THE BRIDE,
BUT FIRST A DETOUR TO MEET THE MOTHER OF THE BRIDE

CHAPTER FOURTEEN

Habakkuk 2:3

For still the vision awaits its appointed time; it hastens to the end—it will not lie. If it seems slow, wait for it; it will surely come; it will not delay.

Back home in the United States, we continued to plan the wedding for Kenol and Lisa. The choir was excited about the idea of singing at the wedding, and the orphanage very excited to host the event. Lisa chose an amazing dress from some pictures I showed her online. I took the picture of her dream wedding dress and posted the picture and some of our story on social media, asking for a size 6 wedding dress. I received a phone call the next day from a lady who was in tears. She spoke to me through her tears saying that she had the exact dress we were looking for. She said her daughter had previously been engaged, but something had happened, and her daughter did not get married. She had already purchased the wedding dress, and it had been in storage for two years. She had tried to sell the dress on numerous occasions, but to no avail. She finally realized, upon seeing that post, that God had been saving the dress for just this occasion. The dress still had the price tag on it. It was beautiful, and more than perfect.

Our story of Lisa and Kenol's upcoming nuptials had garnered a following on social media, and we soon had many followers very excited about the wedding. The participants on our upcoming annual Christmas Mission Trip to Haiti were especially excited, because now they would be treasured guests in attendance at the wedding.

We arrived in Haiti, the week of Christmas 2017. The wedding was scheduled for Saturday, December 23rd. Our required meeting with Jeremy, the voodoo priest was set for Friday, December 22nd and, per my previous agreement, had to happen for the wedding to still occur. On Thursday evening, we confirmed with his daughter Lisa that we'd meet with Jeremy at the orphanage at 12:00 noon.

We had a mission team of 25 people in Haiti that week and a lot on the schedule for the entirety of our trip. Friday morning came, and before we knew it, 12:00 noon had come and gone. Because of traffic and other issues along the way, I had missed our scheduled meeting with Jeremy! Paul William contacted us and told us that Jeremy had been sitting outside the orphanage in a vehicle waiting, but he had just come inside and said he was no longer willing to wait. I slipped away from the rest of the mission team and raced to the orphanage. However, by the time I got there, no one was there. I had Paul William reach out to Lisa and Kenol, and I told them we still needed to figure out a way to make this meeting happen today. I had a driver and an interpreter, so I was willing to travel. Lisa and Kenol agreed to meet me at the orphanage. I waited for them there.

When Lisa arrived, she was distraught. She sat down, and through the interpreter, she explained to me that her mother was very, very sick. She wanted to know if we could go see her mother and asked if I would be willing to pray for her mother. I reiterated how important the timing was. I didn't know the logistics or the distance between where we were and where we had to go to get to Jeremy. Where her mom fit into all that was still unknown. I asked the interpreter once we were all in the truck heading out to please be sure Lisa understood that if we didn't meet with her dad tonight, the wedding was off tomorrow. She was crying and said she understood, but that it was more important that we went to pray for her mom. She felt like we would have time to do both.

I looked at Lisa directly in her eyes, and asked her that if her mom had been sick for so long, why she hadn't just used a voodoo spell to heal her. Lisa's face was in shock. She didn't even seem to understand my question and responded back through the interpreter. "Oh Mommy Linda, don't you remember when you were here in October? I gave my life to Jesus. I don't and I can't do that anymore." The interpreter said, "Linda, I really don't think you grasp how serious it is for a voodoo worshiper to renounce their worship of Satan and turn to Jesus. It is a very serious decision, one that can bring death threats. Once they have renounced voodoo, they would never do that again."

To this day, I still do not know where we went. I've always been told that City Soliel is one of the most dangerous places you can go in Haiti. However, where we went was worse than anything I had ever seen. Our driver stopped the truck on the side of the road, based on

Lisa and Kenol's directions. The four of us got out of the truck, but the driver stayed. So, it was me and our interpreter, Wilno, along with Lisa and Kenol. We walked down a very narrow concrete walkway that looked almost like a tunnel. I realized at this moment there was no turning back. If anything happened to me down here, no one would ever find me. Every three or four feet, we took another step down. It also got darker and darker. By the seventh or eighth step going down, I felt like we were walking down the steps in route to hell. I had left my cell phone in the truck for fear it would be stolen from me. I was desperately wishing I had it with me because there was no light.

After what I recall being the 10th or 15th step down, Lisa and Kenol turned left into a doorway. It was pitch black. Kenol grabbed what looked like a mason jar and lit a match to light a candle. Once the candle was lit, I could see around the room. There was a full-size bed pushed up against the wall in front of us. Along the right side of the bed there was a two-foot space between the bed and the wall. That wall had a broken refrigerator in the corner. On the opposite wall, the one with the door we just entered, there was a table with two chairs. Beyond that, I didn't see anybody. Lisa jumped up on the bed and looked down on the floor. She called, "Mom?" I was struggling to see, but I saw Lisa look down on that two-foot gap between the bed and the wall. Her mom was laying on the floor in that small gap. I laid face down on the bed so I could hang over the edge where her mom was laying. Wilno, our translator, was telling me the story in English as Lisa and her mother continued to speak in Creole. While we were all talking, Kenol was trying to hold the jar with the candle in it over me so I could see. He ended up just putting the candle on the floor beside the refrigerator.

Lisa's mom, according to Lisa and Kenol, had been laying on the floor for 8 days. She hadn't eaten or gone to the bathroom during that time, and her stomach was understandably radiating with pain. They had taken her to the hospital earlier, on a motorcycle, otherwise known as a "tap-tap," which is a popular mode of public transportation in Haiti. They were trying to find out why Lisa's mother was suffering from such lethargy. Her mom was refused help at the hospital because they didn't have the 100 goudes the hospital required for the assessment, which amounts to less than $2 USD.

The motor bike was the only transportation they could afford to get Lisa's mom to and from the hospital, and on the trip home, she suffered a burn to her leg on from the exposed muffler. Kenol tried to hold the light over Lisa's mom's leg to show me what looked like a banana with its skin peeled back. He finally pulled her leg up in the air for me to see it. You could see the raw skin and open sores. Lisa's mom returned home far worse than when she originally left for the hospital.

This whole scenario was heartbreaking, and based on where I was, I should have been scared to death. However, I had absolutely no fear. The last 30 days of my life had prepared me for such a time as this. I laid down on the bed and hung over the edge. I placed my hands on Lisa's mom who was still laying on the concrete floor. I prayed. Less than a minute later, she sat up on the floor. I asked Kenol to bring the chair from the table and wedge it into the two-foot gap. He did and Lisa's mom got up of her own strength and sat in the chair. She looked very lovingly in my eyes and said, "Mwen grangou," which means, "I'm hungry." I said, "I hear ya' girlfriend! What do you want to eat?" She wanted some chicken. "We can make that happen!"

We left Lisa's mom sitting in a chair, and headed up the same steps we descended earlier, the only way to get back to the truck. Someone had come into the room to stay with Lisa's mom. As I was climbing back up those cold, dark, wet, moldy, concrete stairs, with every step I took, I was thanking and praising God for the miracle He had just performed. We made it to the top of the stairs, and it was dark, even outside of the tunnel. We took a young man with us, and bought a plate of chicken and rice and beans on the side of the road. He then left us and rode a motorbike back to take the food to Lisa's mom. We headed up the mountain to where we hoped to find Jeremy. About 25 minutes later, Lisa received a call. Her mother had already eaten the plate of food we purchased for her and was able to use the bathroom. Unbelievable! Lisa believed if we went to her mother to pray, her mom would be healed, and she was.

We drove through the busy Friday night traffic for almost two hours. When we finally pulled off the main road, there was no light to be found, not even the headlights from passing cars. It was very dark. I asked the driver to leave the headlights on so we could see where we were going to be walking. Even in the darkness, I could see that we had pulled into a place that looked like it used to be a very large home. However, much of the building was in ruins and there was no roof. The ground was covered in concrete and steps. I thought that we must be in a home that had been destroyed by the earthquake. As we were walking up to the house in the dark, Kenol called out Jeremy's name. Someone came walking toward us, but I couldn't see a thing. We were out of the range of the truck's headlights. I am totally convinced that Haitians can see in the dark. But this white girl couldn't see anything.

I was hanging on to the arm of my interpreter, Wilno, and following him with every step we took.

I heard some noises, and then someone struck a match and lit a candle. It resembled one of those short white candles that churches sometimes hand out at Christmas Eve services. However, this one didn't have that little white circular cuff to protect your hand from dripping wax. With the candle lit, I could see a lady carrying out several high back dining room chairs, setting them in a circle on the rocky, uneven concrete for us to sit down. And then I saw a man with gray hair wearing a black bulky leather jacket and jeans. He was holding the candle. Lisa introduced me to her father, Jeremy. He had a very big smile on his face and handed me the candle. He told me to sit down. He reminded me of someone you might see sitting around a fire at a cabin in the woods. He looked much bigger than he really was because of the bulky, leather jacket he was wearing. The one thing he did not look like, however, was a voodoo priest. We all sat down in the chairs the lady had placed in a circle. As I moved the candle around, I could see empty liquor bottles laying around on the concrete floor. Jeremy looked at me and spoke to me in Creole, as if I understood everything he was saying. Wilno would interpret. Jeremy knew our meeting was a condition for me to proceed with the wedding for his daughter the next day. I started the conversation through the interpreter and apologized for not being at the orphanage earlier that day. I thanked him for going to the orphanage, and I thanked him for allowing us to come to his home. "Pa ge pwoblem, Pa ge pwoblem," he laughed, repeating himself several times, saying, "No problem." He continued, "What is it that you want from me? I am happy to do whatever you want me to do."

I noticed the candle dripping wax on my hand, but I couldn't feel it burning me. I just kept holding it up so Jeremy could see my face and I could see his. I told him I wanted to meet him because of the problems we were having in America with some of the choir children. He told me that Lisa and Kenol had informed him about the girls being sick. He said he was so sorry they were not feeling well. I told him his daughter was getting married tomorrow, and we really wanted him to come to the wedding. He said he would be happy to come. He smiled and laughed throughout the entire conversation. Then I told him the main reason I wanted to meet him was that I wanted to introduce him to Jesus Christ. He called to a lady in another part of the house, and she brought him a Bible. He laughed and smiled and told me he knew Jesus. He started quoting scripture after scripture. The more he laughed, the more I started to smell alcohol. I finally realized the alcohol I was smelling was not from the empty bottles laying around, but it was rather from Jeremy. He said he knew I wanted him to do something with Jesus, and if I told him what I wanted him to do, he would do it. Then he started laughing even louder. I looked at Wilno, the interpreter, and said, "Jeremy is smashed, he's absolutely drunk!" Wilno agreed with me. I told Jeremy I really wanted him to come to his daughter's wedding the next day, and I would look forward to seeing him there. Knowing there was no possibility of a productive conversation, I was ready to leave.

As I stood up to depart, Jeremy said, "No, wait, wait! You didn't tell me what you want me to do about God. What do you want me to do so my daughter can get married?" I said, "Nothing, Jeremy. I don't want you to do anything." He kept laughing. Lisa and Kenol looked very disappointed. They were apologizing for how drunk Jeremy was.

You could see the fear in their faces. They were scared that I might not be happy with the results of the meeting with Jeremy, and they feared I might call off the wedding. I handed the candle back to Jeremy and thanked him. I gave him a big hug and told him it was wonderful to meet him. He looked back at me and said, "You see, I am a very nice man, right? You see that? You see I love God, right?" I answered back and told him I was looking forward to seeing him at the wedding the next day. As we were leaving, the lady came back to retrieve all the chairs in the darkness. Jeremy quickly introduced the lady as his wife. I gave her a hug also and then held onto Wilno's arm for security and stability as we walked back to the truck. Lisa and Kenol took a tap-tap back to where they were staying, and I headed back to join the mission team at Pastor Maxeau's home. Tomorrow was a big day. We had a wedding to perform!

THE WEDDING

CHAPTER FIFTEEN

Genesis 2:19

Then the LORD God said, "It is not good that the man should be alone; I will make him a helper fit for him."

The next day was filled with hustle and bustle and last-minute preparations for this unbelievable wedding. We had the dream dress, David had taken Kenol shopping for the perfect groom's suit, and all the children were ready to sing. Everything was perfect! The ladies at the orphanage cooked all day, the aroma of Haitian food is unexplainable. There was so much excitement at the orphanage that day. The kids spent the day decorating. Neighbors came in to do hair and makeup. Lisa was the most beautiful bride. It was at least 100 degrees with no air conditioning, but that didn't put a stop to the day's festivities. While Pastor Maxeau performed the ceremony, I was the maid of honor and Paul from the orphanage stood with the groom. As the time of the official ceremony arrived, the guests began pouring in. Not much of anything in Haiti starts on time, so we continued to wait for the Father of the Bride to make his entrance. We waited and waited. Guests continued to pour in, and the sun began to set. Once we set up generators to have power for lights, Lisa finally said "Let's go ahead without him". My amazing husband stepped in like a champ and proudly took the place of the Father of the Bride. He walked Lisa down the flight of steps to the staging area we had set up for the wedding. The ceremony was perfect. The Haitian orphan children's choir, decked out in their costumes, sang for the ceremony, and it was amazing. The celebration afterwards was a full-blown wedding party. We had a wedding cake, plenty of food and everything was wonderful. Sadly, there was no Jeremy.

Christmas Mission Team in Haiti who were privileged to attend Lisa and Kenols wedding

Samaika, Lisa and Bianca just before the wedding)

CHRISTMAS EVE WITH JEREMY

CHAPTER SIXTEEN

Matthew 28:18-20

Then Jesus came to them and said, "All authority in heaven and on earth has been given to me. Therefore, go and make disciples of all nations, baptizing them in the name of the Father and of the Son and of the Holy Spirit, and teaching them to obey everything I have commanded you. And surely, I am with you always, to the very end of the age."

Sundays are always very busy days on Mission Trips in Haiti. There is usually a two- to-four-hour drive to get to the church from the guest house. This particular Sunday was the day after the big wedding celebrating Kenol and Lisa, with our team joining the reception to celebrate the newlyweds. Following the church service, we had a huge Christmas party scheduled at the Hope and Love orphanage. We always brought Christmas Joy Bags prepared by volunteers in America. They'd make their way to Haiti, where we'd hand them out to the children at the orphanages, schools and churches supported by Love Him

Love them in Haiti. It doesn't matter how many joy bags we bring to Haiti, we never have enough.

We had the Mission team preparing for the party at the orphanage, expecting once again that we would have more children than gifts. Apparently, word had spread throughout the neighborhood about our team hosting a Christmas party at the orphanage, because as we were inside the orphanage setting up, the number of children waiting outside continued to multiply. For every Christmas event we have in Haiti, the children from the orphanage or school sing for us and perform a Christmas skit. It is always a very entertaining highlight. That day's Christmas party was no exception. We continued to prepare the food, gifts and set up the sound system, and the children continued to pour into the orphanage looking for seats.

In the middle of all the chaos, Wilno, our interpreter, pulled me aside and said, "Mommy Linda, I really think you should go back to see Jeremy." I could barely hear him with all the noise from the children attending the party. "What, Wilno?" I asked. He said it again, this time speaking directly into my ear. "I really think you should go back and talk to Jeremy again." I motioned for him to walk out on the back patio of the orphanage where it was quieter. "Why do you say that, Wilno?" I asked. He said, "I've been thinking about it, and he was expecting you on Friday night. He knew you were coming. That is why he looked like he did and acted so normal."

Confused, I said, "Wilno, he was drunk. If he was trying to be so normal, why...." Wilno interrupted me. He said, "He was prepared, I just know it. He was hiding all of his voodoo. He didn't want you to know about the voodoo. You need to go back and surprise him. I really think you need to go back. Now." Again, confused by Wilno's insistence, I replied, "We are in the middle of a huge party! And, besides that, it's Christmas Eve! I can't just leave here and show up at a voodoo priest's home. On top of that we are still in trouble with Pastor Maxeau for going to all those places we weren't supposed to go on Friday night. Just forget it." Wilno was very persuasive and insistent. He said, "Go with Pastor Maxeau, take him with you."

When we walked back into the party, it almost seemed like I wasn't really needed there. Everything was chaotic, but the mission team was doing everything that needed to be done to make it all happen. I looked over and saw Wilno. I motioned to him for him to go tell Pastor Maxeau what he told me. He did. Pastor Maxeau made his way through the crowd to me and said, "Mommy Linda, do you want to go back and see Jeremy?" Without another thought, I said, "Sure, let's go."

Pastor Maxeau and I left the orphanage and hopped in his truck. However, Wilno was not with us. I told Maxeau that I really didn't think I could find the place because it was so dark when we had gone before. I asked him if he knew where to go, and he replied with an unworried "No." A little confused, I asked, "How in the world are we going to find where we are going." Pastor Maxeau did not even hesitate. He answered, "Don't worry, Mommy Linda, the Holy Spirit will show us where to go." Less than 15 minutes later we were pulling into the dilapidated broken-down cement building Jeremy called home. As we pulled in, Pastor Maxeau said, "Watch what I am going to do." He turned the truck around and backed in. Apparently having had experience with similar situations, he said, "When you come to these situations when the person may want to kill you before you leave, you make it easy so you can jump in the truck and leave quickly." I just laughed, shook my head and jumped out of the truck.

As we started to walk up the short hill through the broken landscape and pieces of cement, we saw Jeremy sitting on a small, preschool sized chair eating a plate of rice and beans. He looked up and saw me and immediately put his food down and came running toward me. He had on a purple voodoo outfit and what looked like powder all over his face. "Mommy Linda, how are you? Who is this with you?" I wasn't sure how to respond. He acted like we had been friends since first grade. I introduced him to Pastor Maxeau. I think he had forgotten that he was completely dressed in his voodoo garb. There were several children there, along with their mothers. I learned later it was common to bring your children between Christmas Eve and New Year's Day to receive a Devil Shower, otherwise known as a Haitian good luck bath. That explained why the kids were there.

Jeremy had chairs brought over for us, and we sat down. I asked him why he didn't show up for his daughter's wedding the day before. He had no answer. I told him I was very disappointed in him, that he hadn't come. As I began telling him what a beautiful ceremony it was, I pulled out my phone to show the pictures. He kept looking at the pictures and saying how nice everything looked. And then I asked, "Do you realize because you weren't there for your daughter's wedding, my husband had to take your place to give your daughter away?" I showed him the picture of my husband walking his daughter down the steps. I was just about to continue scolding him for him not being there, but I realized the moment he laid eyes on my husband taking his place, he completely broke down. To my surprise, he was actually crying. Before I could speak the words, "You should have been there," he said, "I should have been there."

The actual picture I showed Jeremy from my phone of my husband David taking his place walking his daughter down the "aisle" to give her away

I paused for a moment to take in the grief on Jeremy's face. I said, "Jeremy, the reason I came back tonight was the same reason I came the other night. It has nothing to do with bribery, and it's not about the deal for me to pay for your daughter's wedding. You should know that by now because the wedding was yesterday. I already did what I promised. All I really wanted was the opportunity to present Jesus Christ to you. Well, and I curiously want to know why you are performing voodoo." Not fully understanding, he replied, "I told you I would do whatever you wanted me to the other night so my daughter could have a wedding." Again, I responded, "I don't want you to do anything because I want you to do it. I want you to change your life."

I said, "Look around you. This place is horrible. Why in the world would you continue this way? I could understand if you were living in a beautiful house, or if you had nicer belongings, or any reason really. I don't see any reason you would do what you do, practicing voodoo. I can't figure it out." He looked at me and said, "Linda, I know Jesus, I know the Bible. But I can't surrender my life to him." Questioning, I asked, "WHY NOT?" All of this was being partially translated by Maxeau because my Creole was still a little shaky. Jeremy answered, "Because Voodoo is how I make my living. If I surrender my life to Jesus today, how will I eat tomorrow?"

When sharing the gospel in a third world country like Haiti, this question had become unsurprisingly common. "Will your god put food in my belly? Will he put a roof over my head?" My answer to Jeremy was the same as my answer to everyone else in Haiti. I replied, "Jeremy, you really don't think God can provide for you? God sent me here to tell you that He can provide. God can provide through me. If you could start any other business in the world tomorrow, what would it be?" He paused and thought and then responded, "I would be really good at selling liquor! I already have a great customer base for that, and many people will buy from me." I busted out laughing. "I don't think that would be an amazing business for you to be in. Let's talk about faith and how God does provide. Because if the only reason you are on Satan's team is because of how you think Satan is providing for you..."

Pastor Maxeau interrupted me and, in Creole, spoke directly with Jeremy for five minutes without pause. When the men finished speaking, and with a nod from Pastor Maxeau, I asked again if Jeremy was ready to give his life to Christ. I asked if he was ready to see what

God could do. Jeremy took off the voodoo hat. He got out of his chair, dropped to his knees on the concrete, bowed his head and raised his hands to heaven. He prayed on his own, with neither Maxeau nor I leading him. He then began to strip off his clothing. ALL THE WAY DOWN TO HIS UNDERWEAR. He was singing and stripping off everything that clothed and adorned his body related to the voodoo. He was singing and crying and praying. It was an unbelievable and glorious sight!

After about 30 minutes of Jeremy's praises to God, he stood up and immediately led his voodoo assistant, who had been right by his side practicing voodoo for over 15 years, to salvation through Jesus Christ. The next thing I knew, his assistant was on his knees praying and worshiping God. Jeremy told his assistant if they could worship Satan together, they needed to take this next step together to worship Jesus. I REALLY couldn't believe it. In America, most people end up taking three or four months of discipleship classes before they are willing to share the gospel. It took Jeremy three minutes!

Jeremy guided Pastor Maxeau and me over to another section of the house, where there were two rooms completely full of voodoo paraphernalia previously used for their spells and curses. Maxeau said all of it had to go. We started cleaning out the room. We started a fire and just kept piling all this stuff on the fire. The little kids, originally there for their devil showers, started helping us as we made multiple trips, taking all the skulls and crosses and spices and I don't even know what half of it was, over to the fire, where we watched it burn. It took twenty-five of us almost an hour to clean out everything.

As we watched the fire burn, two of the mothers who were there for their children's Devil showers from Jeremy, said if Jesus was good enough for Jeremy to change, they both wanted Jesus also. While we were praying with these two women, Jeremy received a phone call from someone wanting voodoo services. He sang and shouted on the phone and told them he had something better now and he would no longer be able to help the customer on the phone with voodoo. I was witnessing a complete transformation before my eyes. As the fire continued to burn, we went back to the two empty rooms that had previously housed the voodoo materials needed to perform curses and spells. They were horrible, filling us with an indescribable feeling of an eerie evil I can't fully communicate. Dark, moldy, roaches crawling on the wall, wet... JUST NASTY! We prayed over the rooms and asked God to completely cleanse them. When we finished praying in the second room, a white dove flew in the opening over the door. The sound of its wings flying in scared me to death, and when I saw what it was, I was overwhelmed. The presence of the Holy Spirit was there with us. It was an evening that will forever be with me.

Back to business, Pastor Maxeau said we needed to get back to our Christmas Eve party at the orphanage. He told Jeremy we would return the next day to discuss ways we could help him move forward. Maxeau told me to give Jeremy some money so he could have food for Christmas Day. With his thick Haitian accent, he said, "Mommy Linda, the gospel is free but evangelism cost money!" With a laugh, I gave Jeremy money with which to buy his Christmas dinner. And with hugs all around, we said our good-byes.

The party was winding down when we returned to the orphanage, and the whole team asked where we had been. We waited

Within minutes of Jeremy surrendering his life to Christ, he led his assistant to Jesus with the help of Pastor Maxeau

A few of the items that came out of the room Jeremy used to perform voodoo rituals

Jeremy on his knees praising God, directly behind him in the white dress is his daughter Lisa

The fire burning all of the voodoo paraphernalia from Jeremy's voodoo ceremony room. Can you see the demons face in the fire? If not, look at the close up version in the next picture

When I showed this picture of the fire to some of the children in the choir whose families involved them in voodoo ceremonies, they actually recognized this demon and said they had seen him at many ceremonies coming up out of the fire when they burned alcohol. When I looked closer at the video of the fire, it was when a box of liquor was thrown on the fire this face appeared.

Can you see the difference between Jeremy BEFORE JESUS and AFTER JESUS?

until we returned to the guest house for the night and shared the story. EVERYONE wanted to go back with us the next day to meet Jeremy. So that's exactly what we did. The group of us piled into the cattle truck, and we were off to see Jeremy. During the drive, a part of me was hesitant, thinking, "What if it was all an act? What if we pull up and he's not there? Or worse, what if we arrive and he is doing voodoo?" Rather than allowing this uncertainty to take over, I directed my attention back to the mission team, and my thoughts back to the joyful anticipation of seeing Jeremy again today.

When we arrived, Maxeau pulled straight in, saying, to the utter confusion of the team, he felt we were safe now that no one would try to kill us. With a laugh, I thanked him for the assurance. Everyone was so excited and climbed up the broken concrete to get to where Jeremy and his "wife" were. Some of the women and children were still there from the night before. Jeremy looked like a completely different man. No alcohol had touched his lips since we saw him the night before, and he wasn't in is his voodoo ceremony outfit. He just looked radiant. We sat and talked about his future. We offered him a business opportunity, and we also suggested he "change his playground" (move to a different home in a different community). He was too well known in the area where he resided, and everyone would continue to come there for his services. We also spent some time counseling with him. We learned the lady he was calling his wife was not actually his wife. We learned he had children with over 14 women, possibly more. After explaining that if he was going to cohabitate, he needed to commit himself to one woman only and get married -- so he did. (The woman he married wasn't the one he was living with in his current home.) We went and met with the woman Jeremy wanted to marry. She was a voodoo princess who had also practiced voodoo. Jeremy told her that he wanted to marry her to her great excitement.

It was Christmas Day, and Pastor Maxeau was due to pastor at our church in a nearby town called Doco, a church that was newly constructed through the support of the Love Him Love Them ministry. All of us, including Maxeau, myself, the mission team, Jeremy, and his intended, set off for church. During the service, Maxeau brought Jeremy up in front of the church, introducing him to the whole congregation, sharing Jeremy's entire story. Maxeau explained that Jeremy would be moving to the area, and he wanted everyone in the church to hold Jeremy accountable. I couldn't believe it. Then at the end of the service, Maxeau presented the gospel, and the woman who came with Jeremy surrendered her life to Jesus Christ. It was an overwhelming experience.

The next day, we went back to the place where Jeremy's intended was living, and just as we had with Jeremy, we explained to her that

Mommy Linda, Sarah and Jeremy's intended on the way to church in Haiti

*Jeremy, Mommy Linda Jeremy's intended
and Mr. David at Church*

Pastor Maxeau introducing Jeremy at church

all of the voodoo paraphernalia would have to go. She had a room set up that was just as horribly dark and dreary as Jeremy's. We began cleaning it out. Her 13-year-old daughter was helping us, and as we were sweeping out the last of the liquor bottles, her daughter asked if she could make Jesus the Lord of her life. Standing in the room where her mom had performed voodoo spells, just a few days earlier, she surrendered her live to Jesus Christ! Standing in a room that held so much evil, we were now basking in the Lord's glory and light. It was unbelievable!

Over the coming days, we counseled Jeremy and his intended, sharing with them what a godly marriage looked like. After a lot

Right after their daughter surrendered her life to Jesus in the same room her mom previously performed voodoo ceremonies L-R Jeremy, their daughter, Jeremy's intended, Redaphca , Sarah, Mommy Linda and Pastro Maxeau)

(Jeremy's intended in front of all the voodoo paraphernalia we removed from the room she performed her spells)

The items she used in voodoo ceremonies now burning and gone forever

of consideration, they broke off their engagement. We moved to the next woman Jeremy had on his list of 14. It took us about three months total, but we moved Jeremy to a new home. Jeremy continued attending the church in Doco, and still attends services there, to this day. The second woman he chose ended up being his bride. They had a beautiful wedding at the church with their newfound church family. This is not the ending to this story that I would have ever imagined, but God had such different plans. Where I could only see evil, God had plans to turn it into good. God taught me an important lesson in that season about what it is to boast in the hope of the glory of God. Under my own power, Jeremy was as good as dead. Christ dies for the ungodly, and that included the voodoo practicing, curse wielding, spell casting Jeremy. As we are reminded in Romans 6:8… "BUT God demonstrates his own love for us in this: While we were still sinners, Christ died for us."

SONSAY'S STRUGGLE

CHAPTER SEVENTEEN

Ecclesiastes 3:1-4

For everything there is a season, and a time for every matter under heaven: a time to be born, and a time to die; a time to plant, and a time to pluck up what is planted; a time to kill, and a time to heal; a time to break down, and a time to build up; a time to weep, and a time to laugh; a time to mourn, and a time to dance

I received a message from Haiti that one of the children from the choir, a nine-year-old boy named Sonsay, was sick. The directors of the orphanage said they had been treating him at the orphanage but decided to take him to a hospital. The description passed along to me was that the boy seemed to have a bad cold. I asked if I could help in any way, and was told they just wanted to let me know. I explained that I was accompanying a Mission Team heading down to Haiti that following week, so we would come to the hospital upon arrival to check on him and see how we could help the young boy.

I flew to Haiti the next week with a group of college girls, who were all friends of Sarah Logan, who had joined us at Mother

Emmanual Church when our group sangthere during our 2016 concerrt tour. By this time, Sarah was serving as a full-time ministry intern on the ground in Haiti. The day after we arrived in Haiti, we went to the hospital to see Sonsay, the sick boy we had heard about. When I first laid eyes on Sonsay, I had to leave the room to regain my composure. He was lying on a urine-stained bed in the "ICU" for children, which was nothing more than a lineup of beds in a long cinderblock room. Each bed contained a sick child, and there were no partitions or dividers to be seen. Sonsay's head had been partially shaved, and he looked horrible. I sat with Sonsay, and talked with him. He was VERY weak. I stepped out to try and speak with a nurse or doctor, to find out what was going on, but I couldn't find anyone there who spoke English. I reserved a few minutes of the doctor's time for the next day, so I could learn more about Sonsay's condition. As I departed, one of the older girls from the orphanage arrived to sit with Sonsay throughout the night.

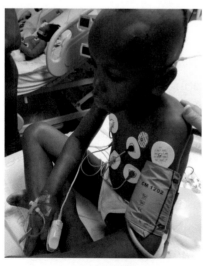

Sonsay in the hospital

I returned to the hospital the next day to meet with the doctor. I learned Sonsay needed blood, but that was all the information the doctor had for me. I asked, "Do you need some sort of consent to give him blood?" "No", the doctor replied, "we don't need consent, but we do need the blood." Coming from America, with a blood supply readily available at our hospitals,

I questioned, "Excuse me? You need blood? Do you not have blood here at the hospital?" The doctor answered, "No, ma'am; blood has to be obtained from the Red Cross." I stared at the doctor very confused and then asked, "And where is the Red Cross?" "It will take you about an hour to get to the closest location," was his reply, quickly adding, "depending on traffic."

I stood up and began to walk out the door with every intent to navigate my way to the Red Cross. I paused, and then turned back to ask the doctor if I would need any formal order or instructions from the hospital to get the blood. He looked back at me, and his next words were some of the strangest instructions I had ever been given. He said, "They won't just give you blood. You will need to take at least three people with you to give blood first, and then if they have blood, they should give you blood." I just stood in the doorway staring at the doctor. And then he added, "Oh, and ma'am, don't forget, you'll need to take a cooler with you." "A cooler?" I asked. "Yes, the cooler is what you will use to bring the blood back to the hospital." I started to blurt out, "You have got to be kidding me, right?!" But I could see that he was very serious, and I kept my mouth shut. I hurried out the door to find my driver, and begin the journey of figuring out how to get the blood.

Fortunately, I had a mission team with me, so I didn't have to go into the streets to find three people willing to give blood. The first step was to find a store and buy a cooler. While I was shopping for the cooler, another driver was maneuvering through the congested traffic of Haiti, bringing three of our mission team members to The Red Cross, where we'd meet up. Three hours later, we had all arrived at the Red Cross office, and we began our wait. There were at least 75 people in line, ahead of us, and everyone was waiting with an empty cooler, and it was a very strange situation. We completed the paperwork, and then we waited... and waited... and waited. By the time we were called to go back and give blood, the place was overrun with hundreds of people. We never had a chance to give blood, because they closed the office before it was our turn. We were simply told we could come back the next day and start the process all over again. That same message was passed along down the line to all the other people waiting behind us. The despair on everyone's faces was unmistakable.

The actual cooler we used to take to the Red Cross to get blood and platelets for Sonsay

The team members returned to the guest house, and I went back to the hospital. Talking with a nurse, I described our trip to The Red Cross, and explained that were had been turned away without the blood we needed for Sonsay. The nurse then explained to us that

Sonsay needed platelets, not blood. Hesitantly, I asked, "Where do you get platelets?" "But of course, The Red Cross," she answered. "Of course, The Red Cross," I mumbled -- the Red Cross, where we had sat all day, waiting, the very one that was now closed.

I spent some time speaking with other people who were at the hospital. I could not help but wonder how everyone else was getting blood and platelets and yet still able to stay by the bedside of their loved ones. I learned that the key to the system was paying someone to go and be the first person in line the next day. I paid, gave them my cooler and agreed to meet them back at the hospital the next day.

I arrived at the hospital early the next morning. I was in the lobby speaking with the doctor when, 10 minutes later, my "platelet provider" arrived. We could see him from the open-air lobby as he jumped off the back of a moto-bike tap-tap and walked into the lobby with the cooler. He went to hand me the cooler, and the doctor asked him something in Creole. The young man responded by shaking his head back and forth no. The doctor looked at me and said, "When you get platelets, they have to be shaken the entire time, from the moment you receive them until the moment you deliver them to the hospital. Otherwise, they are no good." The platelet delivery man just hung his head low and handed me the cooler. Frustrated, I walked upstairs with the doctor to see Sonsay. He looked worse. I kept asking the doctor what was wrong with him, and no one could give an answer. It was obvious that Sonsay was not getting any better.

I stayed at the hospital that day, where I watched Sonsay slowly decline. I heard some conversations at the nurse's station that indicated that Sonsay had Typhoid Fever. I knew NOTHING about typhoid but started searching for information on my phone. I learned it was treatable. I asked the nurses that afternoon about helping Sonsay with the treatment. There was a language barrier, and they weren't able to respond to me.

I could no longer sit by idly, watching Sonsay decline with neither answers nor treatment in sight. I started calling hospitals in America to see if they could treat Sonsay. However, without a visa, we'd be unable to bring him to the United States for treatment. For the next 24 hours, I did everything I could to get Sonsay an emergency medical visa. I filled out the general visa paperwork, and I made four trips to the US Embassy, where I was ultimately told there was no such thing as a Medical Emergency Visa. With a firm, "No," I was told it would take up to three months to arrange a visa, and for the final assessment, I'd have to bring Sonsay to the embassy. However, with Sonsay lying in a hospital bed five miles away from the Embassy, barely able to breathe, I knew there was no way he would be able to make the trip. I was fighting for this boy's life. Standing on the other side of a glass partition with tears streaming down my face, I did my best to explain the situation again to the interviewer at the embassy. After one final, "No," I was emotionally and physically exhausted. I broke down and sobbed. I looked at the embassy worker through the glass, and said one final time, "If this boy does not get proper treatment within the next 24 hours, he is going to die!" And then she finally gave me the smallest sliver of hope and said if I could get a written note from the doctors at the hospital explaining that Sonsay would be unable to travel to the Embassy, maybe they could do something.

I had our volunteers in America begin making calls to figure out flights and a hospital that would accept Sonsay. I raced back to the hospital. All the doctors had already left the hospital for the day, so I went to Sonsay's bed, where I sat with him, held his hand, and prayed.

Bright and early the next morning, I requested a piece of paper from the doctor that explained Sonsay's condition, as the Embassy worker had requested. I received that I needed, and headed off for the embassy. Having seen me pass through many times by now, the security guard posted outside the embassy just let me pass through the line and go inside. I handed the paper to the interviewer, who told me she would do what she could. I was instructed to check back at four o'clock that afternoon. Now, we still needed to find a hospital in America that would accept Sonsay. Having deteriorated to a point where he was unable to breathe on his own, a regular airline would not allow Sonsay to fly. We faced the challenge of finding a private medical plane that would be willing to fly Sonsay to the United States. And again, for this, we had to have a hospital in America willing to take him. After spending two days on the phone, calling one hospital after another – with the help of a few friends, doing the same thing -- we finally found a hospital in the U.S. willing to take Sonsay. Their only request was to have a phone conversation with the doctors from the hospital in Haiti to assess his condition. The call was arranged, and for the first time in days, I began to feel a sense of relief, as everything seemed to be falling into place. Halfway there, I just needed the emergency medical visa and private medical plane to come through.

At four o'clock, I headed back to the US Embassy, and again walked straight in. When I stepped up to the window, I was told that "miraculously" (that was the word the interviewer used) the visa had been approved, and I could come back first thing the next morning to retrieve it. I returned to the hospital to share the amazing news that we had the medical visa, and I called the hospital in America to let them know we would soon be on our way. The hospital asked to speak with the doctor in charge of the ICU to get an update on Sonsay. The doctor in charge at that moment was a female doctor who was not very fond of me. (To this day, I am not sure what I ever said or did to upset her.) I asked her if she would be willing to speak to the hospital in America, and she smiled and said, "Sure." I handed her my phone, and she asked me to step outside of the ICU. I was so excited and happy about getting the medical visa, I obediently stepped out.

Waiting just outside of the ICU, I was thanking God for lining everything up. The director of the orphanage showed up at the hospital, and I began sharing all the exciting news with him, as we waited together. We were both so happy, praising God for paving the way down a seemingly impossible path. A short time later, the female doctor in charge of the ICU stepped outside to join me and our orphanage director, and she handed my phone back to me. The doctor smiled and said, "The hospital wants to speak with you." I grabbed the phone and said, "Yes, this is Linda."

What I heard next I still can't fully comprehend. Completely blindsided, I truly cannot explain to you fully what I heard on the other side of the call. I was thrust into a state of shock. The nurse from the hospital in America was yelling through the phone and instructed me to never call her hospital in America again. She told me I was despicable, and she couldn't believe what a horrible person I was to stoop so low as to steal a child away from his parents in Haiti, to take him to America. The lady never took a breath, and I never had a chance to say a word. She told me the room was no longer available, and that I should never call her or the hospital again, and she abruptly hung up.

The director of the orphanage had been standing beside me the entire time, where he was also able to hear everything coming from the other side of the phone conversation. We immediately walked back into the ICU to ask the female doctor what in the world she said to the American hospital. She wouldn't look at me, but spoke directly to the orphanage director in Creole, telling him we could no longer be in the ICU, advising us to leave. Standing outside the ICU in shock, we were both plagued with despair, disbelief, confusion, and a newfound sense of hopelessness. I went down to the lobby, where I sat on a bench in the 100-degree weather and cried.

When I was finally coherent enough to wrap my head around everything that had happened, I recalled having made an acquaintance who ran an ambulance service in Haiti. I called her and explained the whole story, and her first comment to me was, "You need to get that boy out of that hospital." She continued, "There are other hospitals here that could have already treated him. I'll send an ambulance to get him right now, and we can put him somewhere that may be able to help him." Miraculously, she also said she had three different connections with operators of medical planes, and the minute we had approval from a hospital in America that would take him, we could fly Sonsay out. I asked how much the ambulance would cost to transport him to another hospital, and she said, "Nothing, but the medical plane will be a minimum of $25,000." I said "Okay, make it happen," and then hung up the phone.

I didn't say a word to anyone. I was terrified that if the female doctor knew an ambulance was coming to the hospital to retrieve

Sonsay, she may.... well, I didn't know what she'd do. I had no idea where to get the needed $25,000 to fly Sonsay out of Haiti, and now we were back at square one trying to find another hospital in America that would accept him. The quality of my phone service in Haiti wasn't strong enough for me to make calls to American hospitals, so I once again recruited the help of friends in America to make the calls. When I told my friends about the shocking turn of events with the hospital that was originally willing to take Sonsay, they called and tried to speak with the nurse who told me never to call back, but she refused to take their calls.

At this point in time, my mind was spinning. Sonsay was lying in an ICU bed in the children's ward of a hospital in Haiti, a ward that I was now prohibited from entering. We miraculously managed to get him a medical emergency visa, and just needed to pick it up the next morning from the embassy in Haiti. We had three medical flights available to us at the cost of $25,000 – which, as of that moment, we did not have. But first, we had to find another hospital in America ready and willing to accept Sonsay – and the doctors from that hospital would need to speak to the doctors currently treating him in Haiti, before we could arrange to have him released for the trip to the U.S. It was clear that we needed to move Sonsay to another hospital in Haiti, in order to have him under the care of a Haitian doctor who would approve his transport to the U.S. We had an ambulance on the way to the hospital where Sonsay was lying in an ICU bed -- yet, we were not allowed into the ICU to simply sweep him off to another hospital in Haiti. I went back to the downstairs lobby and prayed. I prayed for God to find us the $25,000 we needed for Sonsay's medical flight to the U.S. I asked God to prevent the female doctor upstairs not to kill me or Sonsay, when she saw the ambulance coming to get him. I prayed for Sonsay to be completely healed. I prayed that all my friends calling various hospitals in America, seeking one that would agree to accept Sonsay, would be successful. I asked the Holy Spirit to speak to the lady who had just reamed me out on the phone, asking him to speak the truth to her. Mostly, I prayed that my friend in Haiti who said she was sending an ambulance, with another hospital in Haiti at the ready, was really going to come through and make it all happen. And then I sat and stared, watching the front of the hospital, waiting on an ambulance to arrive. Time stood still.

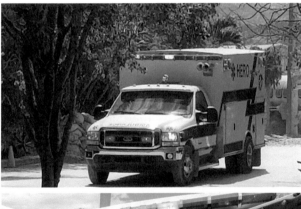

The ambulance pulling up to hospital to get Sonsay

Loading Sonsay in ambulance

As I watched, an ambulance with a Haitian driver pulled up in the front of the hospital, and two American EMT's stepped out and said, "Hi Linda, we came to get Sonsay!" Grateful to see their faces, I told them he was upstairs. They pulled out a stretcher, rolled it up the ramp and walked right into the ICU. They quickly introduced themselves to the female doctor and immediately started hooking Sonsay up to an IV and transferred him onto the stretcher. Miraculously, in less than ten minutes, Sonsay was in the back of the ambulance, and we were on our way to... well, I had no idea where. They let me ride along in the ambulance, and it was like a breath of fresh air that once again brought me hope. I could hear my friend speaking to the EMT's on the radio, telling them where to go.

We pulled up to a building, where we waited outside a metal door that was quickly opened by a security guard. I saw the word "Hospital" on a metal plaque. They took Sonsay directly into a room where they began treatment. I don't know the details of what they treated him with, but I do know this... they were nice, VERY NICE. So nice. Did I say they were nice? The hospital was staffed by a team of American and Haitian doctors and nurses. We started to explain the whole story, and the doctors said they already had all the information they needed, to treat Sonsay, having spoken with staff at the other hospital. They were going to run some tests and see where to go from there. My phone rang, and it was my friends in America giving me an update that the $25,000 we needed for Sonjay's medical transport flight had been donated -- and in addition, we had three pilots from America offer to come over and get Sonsay. We still had not found a hospital in the U.S. that would accept him, however.

A little later, the mission team of girls showed up at the new hospital, and were excited to see Sonsay. With an infusion of platelets, fluids, and medication, he sat up for the first time in days and asked for some food. The girls went out into the streets, where they purchased his favorite juice and some rice. He looked so much better. It crossed my mind he might even be able to fly on a commercial flight at this point if we could just get him past the need for oxygen. After a trying day, some people from the orphanage came to stay with Sonsay overnight, and I went back to the guest house to rest.

The next morning, I went straight to the Embassy to pick up Sonsay's Medical Visa. It was ready and waiting for me, and the lady at the Embassy cried when she handed me the Visa through the opening in the glass. She told me she could only hope to have an advocate like me fighting for her, if she ever needed help. I cried too and thanked her, and then I headed back to the hospital.

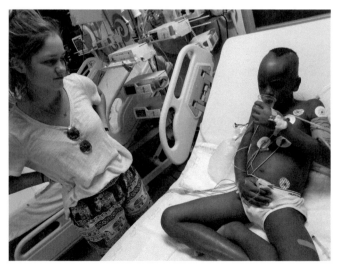

Sarah and Sonsay drinking juice

When I arrived, Sonsay was sitting up, drinking juice and talking. All the girls from the Mission team had beat me to the hospital. He looked so much better. The doctor came in and said that the best thing we could do next was to head to the Red Cross to get more blood for Sonsay. This was not what we wanted to do, but we were all willing. We jumped in the truck, where we fortunately still had our cooler waiting, and headed onced again to the Red Cross – and once again, the entire building was packed with people. We filled out our paperwork and waited. Just looking around the Red Cross lobby is heartbreaking enough – but it's overwhelming to hear the stories of the people there waiting, why they need blood for loved ones, and each person's struggle to finding other people willing to donate blood to accompany them.

It finally was our turn, and the Red Cross staff called us back to the area where they take the blood. This was the first time we had made it this far, in our effort to get blood for Sonsay. On our way to the back, my phone rang. It was the hospital. I had horrible service and lost the call. They called again, and once again I lost the call. I headed out to the lobby, as I tried to get better reception. I walked through the crowd of people and made it to an empty chair in the outside lobby and the phone rang again. This time we connected.

"Linda?" I heard.

"Yes, this is Linda" I responded.

"Hi, it's Amy from the hospital. I just wanted to reach out to you, I know the doctor said you were headed to the Red Cross for blood," she said.

"Yes, actually we are here now and just made it back to give the blood," I replied.

What I heard next gutted me. "Okay, well … I don't know how to tell you this, but Sonsay took a turn for the worse, and he is no longer with us. We don't know what happened. It surprised all of us. We are going to keep him here and prepare him for you to be able to see him. Can you head back to the hospital?"

Tears started pouring down my face as I held the phone. "Linda? Are you there?"

I couldn't speak, I just remember my face being wet. Somehow, I must have said yes.

"Do you have a driver, Linda? To bring you back to the hospital?" Again, I must have answered yes.

I don't remember hanging up, but what happened next, I remember as if it were happening now. The lobby where I was sitting was empty. Tears were gently rolling down my face. I looked over, and standing beside the window was what looked like a Hispanic man (not a Haitian) with silky black hair. The sun from the window had a glow shining all around his head. He looked at me as I was crying and began to sing in English, "You are my sunshine, my only sunshine, you make me happy... you'll never know, dear, how much I love you...." I closed my eyes to clear the tears, and when I looked back up, there were people all over the lobby. The angel who had come to comfort me had disappeared. With a lump in my throat, I sat gathering the strength to go into the back where the others were giving blood. I needed to tell them it was no longer necessary, and instead we needed to head back to the hospital.

I got up, trying to think of what to say. I went to Sarah, our intern, and pulled her to the side to explain to her that Sonsay had passed away. She was heartbroken. She sat with the other girls in the bed of the pick-up truck on the ride back to the hospital, and en route, she shared the devastating news of Sonsay's loss. It was news that none of us could comprehend, news that split our hearts wide open, news that created a bond of shared experience, shared trauma, and shared heartbreak that will forever remain. In that moment, none of us would have believed just how much the loss of a young boy's life would change the lives of others forever in Haiti and America.

SONSAY'S SEASON

CHAPTER EIGHTEEN

At Sonsay's funeral, all the children from the orphanage choir sang the Kirk Franklin song, "My Life Is In Your Hands." I had the opportunity to speak and shared the gospel of Jesus Christ to the overflowing church in Haiti. I fully expected that Sonsay would be raised from the dead at his funeral. I prayed and fully believed, without a sliver of doubt, it would happen. In the middle of the service, there was a very loud ruckus, which I was sure was the sound of Sonsay coming to life. But it ended up being a piece of wood that fell from the balcony, causing the commotion. He did not come back to life, but eight people did surrender their lives to the Lord at Sonsay's funeral. After the service the orphanage children and I were all taken to the graveyard on the orphanage bus. While I got off the bus, the children remained onboard. It is not customary for anyone to go to the graveyard in Haiti since the graveyards there are where bodies are stolen and used for zombie and voodoo activity. But I was asked to go into the graveyard, nonetheless. They had just slid Sonsay's casket into a small cement block mausoleum, and they were cementing the small opening closed to hold the casket in place and to prevent the body from being stolen for immoral purposes. I was handed a stick from the ground, and told to use it to write Sonsay's name and birth and death date. With tearstained cheeks, I did.

While I was in Haiti, I learned that people had gathered in America and had a memorial service for Sonsay. I never realized how many people his life had touched. Many of his sponsors, people that loved his smile, and people touched by the way he had prayed for them gathered and mourned his passing. I realized that Sonsay had touched more people for Jesus in his short nine years on this earth than most people do in their lifetime. Email and comments started pouring in. Churches and Sunday School classes had been praying for Sonsay. Many of the host families he had stayed with on the choir tour were overwhelmed by his illness and passing. Everyone seemed to have a story about Sonsay. It was truly hard to believe that this little boy from Haiti had impacted so many people and so many lives.

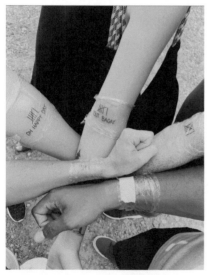

The College Mission Team and friends that Sonsay made a huge impact on had the number 6 tattooed on their arms. 6 was Sonsay's identification number in the choir. They also, each added other words to help them remember Sonsay.

With so many kids on the choir tour, one of the ways we kept track of everyone was with a numbering system. Each child had a number. We would place the number on their clothes and shoes and bags. We also counted off when we got on and off the bus to be sure we had everyone. The numbers ascended from youngest to oldest. Sonsay was number 6.

We later found out about a group of people who had come to Haiti on a Mission Trip who all got a tattoo of the number "6" on their arms to remember Sonsay. There are so many stories like this.

We decided to dedicate the next year's choir tour to Sonsay's memory. We called it "Sonsay's Season." We had a huge poster-size picture of Sonsay in his choir costume and everywhere we sang, we placed the poster on an easel on the stage. That poster is now in my office. At every choir performance, we told Sonsay's story, and we spoke about the hospital we were opening in Haiti, with plans to dedicate the part of the hospital that helped children to Sonsay. Every time we shared Sonsay's story, there was never a dry eye in the audience. While he was no longer on this earth, Sonsay helped raise the majority of the funds to open the hospital. His story was also responsible for multiple salvations.

When we sang at Capstone Church in Anderson, SC and shared the story of Sonsay, a doctor came up to me at the end of the concert. He asked me if I realized that Typhoid fever was completely preventable and there was a vaccine for it? He told me it literally broke his heart to hear the story about Sonsay passing away from something that he has the medicine to treat in his office. I just stood there listening to him as tears rolled down my cheeks. And then he asked if the other children in the choir had been vaccinated for Typhoid fever. Until that very second when he asked me the question I had not even thought of having the other children vaccinated. Feeling akward, I just shook my head no. He said I am going to speak with my colleagues and we are going to figure out how to get the funding to supply you with enough medicine to vaccinate all 30 children. Would that be ok Linda? And that is exactly what he did. All 30 children received the medicine needed to protect them for typhoid fever for a 5 year time frame.

Dr. Shane Purcell sharing with Mommy Linda and Benny Littlejohn (host of WGGST-TV Nite Line in Greenville, SC) about raising the funds to provide typhoid fever medication for all the children in The Love Him Love Them Haitian orphan children's choir

Normil Sonsay · 7

God, I know you added Normil to the choir at the last minute. He is supposedly a substitute for another child. I say Ha Ha! I know this means you have a VERY SPECIAL purpose for him!

Father, completely change Normils life before right now and the end of the tour Lord, show Normil starting today that he is SPECIAL and that we love him and that you love him.

Begin now blessing Normil. Begin preparing him for this summer and the life you have for him. Bless him with the gift of speaking Eng with ease. Gift him with a voice to share your message. Flow through him and allow your words to come off his lips with ease.

Show Normil you love him through the word. He is so young and can use this opportunity to build a strong foundation in you I pray Normil becomes the godly man you have planned for him to be.

God, I pray for Normils purity. I pray for his future wife. Prepare him for her. Keep his eyes always focused on you. Allow him to be a light and a star for Jesus!

I wrote a prayer for each child before I even knew them just from the list of choir names. This was the prayer hanging in my home office for Normil Sonsay

Before the children ever came to America and before I really knew them very well individually, I handwrote a prayer for each of them. I still have the prayer I wrote for Sonsay. I want to share it with you here.

God, I know you added Normil Sonsay to the choir at the last minute. He is supposedly a substitute for another child! I say Ha Ha! I know this means you have a VERY SPECIAL purpose for him.

Father, completely change Normil Sonsay's life between right now and the end of the tour. Lord, show Normil Sonsay, starting today, that HE is special and that we love him and that YOU Love him. Begin now blessing Normil Sonsay. Begin preparing him for this summer and the life you have for him. Bless him with the gift of speaking English with ease. Gift him with a voice to share your message. Flow through him and allow your words to come off his lips with ease.

Show Normil Sonsay you love him through your word. He is so young and can use this opportunity to build a strong foundation in you. I pray now that Normil Sonsay becomes the godly man you have planned for him to be.

God, I pray for Normil Sonsay's purity. I pray for his future wife. Prepare him for her. Keep his eyes always focused on you. Allow him to be a light and a star for Jesus!

Amen.

HOST FAMILIES...
ELDO AND DAVID ALLEN

CHAPTER NINETEEN

James 1:27 (NKJV)

Pure and undefiled religion before God and the Father is this: to visit orphans and widows in their trouble, and to keep oneself unspotted from the world.

At the end of the 2018 tour we titled Sonsay's season, I made the decision that, after touring for three years, if any child in our choir wanted to remain in the United States to continue their education, they would have the opportunity to do so. With student visas in hand, we began the search for host families. It was a difficult process. Bringing a child into your home, and assuming full responsibility for their care and upbringing, is not an easy step. I should know, having taken on the care of eight children and teens over the past 14 years, with four of those eight still living in our home. As international students, the process is even more difficult, with the children needing to attend a private, SEVIS Approved school (meaning the school is approved by Homeland Security to teach international students), which can be costly and difficult to find. Let's just say the entire process of finding host families for each child was something else.... among the many stories that have arisen out of our host families, I want to share just a few.

Eldo, the orphan from Haiti born with six fingers on each hand (who you met earlier in this book), was one of our sweetest boys. Though mischievous at times, (If you ever meet him just ask him about his episode at Stone Mountain, Georgia) Eldo always sported a big smile and ready hugs. Even though everyone who met Eldo loved him, it was much more difficult to find a host home for him than for many of the other children. Like our other older boys, Eldo became accustomed to simply waiting as our cute younger kids were picked by host families first. One family finally stepped up for Eldo, and we were very excited about this. It was a family of a pastor at one of the churches where we sang. We knew and adored this family and they had a special needs son with whom Eldo had a wonderful connection. The placement couldn't have been more perfect.

We were at the end of our tour season and, again, the deadline had arrived for us to be out of the choir house for the summer. It was time for many of the children to return to Haiti, and to arrange the required student visas for others to stay in the United States. Arrangements with host families were still being finalized for some of the remaining kids. As our flight to Haiti quickly approached, I received notice that our originally scheduled flight had been postponed. Having just turned in our keys for the choir house, we once again had to find places for all the kids to stay temporarily. With Eldo's future host family nearby, they let our youngest boy Zackary tag along with Eldo at their home until the time of our flight.

After all the kids were finally settled in local homes, I posted about the postponed flight on social media, and that same day I received a call from a family in Rome, Georgia. They reached out to me, begging me not to send another one of our boys, Davidson, back to Haiti without a home. They felt the delayed flight was their confirmation of a last opportunity to do what they had felt God calling them to do all along. Praising God for having delivered one more home, we arranged the official application and host interview, and identified a SEVIS Approved private school that Davidson would be able to attend.

The following day, I received yet another phone call. It was from the family caring for Eldo and Zackary. Running errands and tying up loose ends before our flight to Haiti the next morning, I spoke with this family during the entirety of the hour drive it took me to get back home. The family was upset about some of the things Zackary had done while at their house. They said it opened their eyes to possible problems they might have with Eldo in the future, and for that reason they could no longer commit to hosting Eldo. Exhausted, I hung up the phone, and went inside to finish packing up for our flight the following day.

That next morning, as we departed for our flight to Haiti, I couldn't decide how I was going to tell Eldo he no longer had a host family in the United States. Rather than telling him this bad news, I decided I would just find him another family. We went back to Haiti – and found ourselves stuck there, as the country was experiencing an extreme bout of civil unrest due to political corruption. With the shutdown of government buildings, it was almost impossible to get into the embassy to finalize student visas for the kids. The riots and street manifestations in Haiti lingered on and on. I booked a single ticket home to Georgia for a brief two days to attend my daughter's graduation from University of North Georgia, and then back down to Haiti I went. Once again, the civil unrest continued, lasting from October through Christmas. Stuck in Haiti, unable to traverse the streets to the airport to make it back home, I missed one of our largest ministry events of the year in our home base of Northeast Georgia, serving thousands of homeless and homebound individuals Thanksgiving Dinner.

Finally, the civil unrest in the streets of Haiti began to settle down, and in early December, we arranged for another mission team to arrive in Haiti. Most of the participants in this group attended the Living Word Church in Maiden, North Carolina. Also in this mission group was a single straggler from another church, David Allen, who was from Dawsonville, Georgia. David attended a very small church named Antioch, a church I had never heard of. It was unusual since I had travelled to or contacted most of the churches in the state of Georgia, during the course of our three-year choir tour. Not having yet met him, I asked how he got connected with our mission team. After a lengthy conversation with him, I learned that David, his wife and his daughter had gone to see the choir that year at one of our church performances. I had no recollection of him, having been absent from that performance, stuck in the hospital with Samaika for three days after a fit of manifestations.

David was a little leery of coming on the trip because he knew he would be the only participant in this mission trip who was not a member of the Living Word Church. He fit in so well with the group that I didn't realize, until the third day of the trip, that David was from a different church. On the next to the last day of the mission trip, we went to the choir's orphanage, where we picked up all the kids to take them to the beach. David sat beside Eldo in the back of the cow truck we use to transport large groups in Haiti. I was sitting across the aisle on the truck facing them during the two-hour trip to and from the beach. On the way back, David Allen put his arm around Eldo and motioned to me. Without speaking a word aloud, he mouthed the words, "Does this young boy have a family?" I shook my head, no. Eldo never even knew the wordless conversation happened.

After a fun day playing together, we dropped the kids off at the orphanage and made our way back to the guest house. David asked me a million and one questions, and said he wanted to be Eldo's forever family. In the words of a wise man, he let me know he just felt like he needed to call his wife first to be sure. When we walked into the guest house, he used the limited phone service and placed a call to his wife to announce he wanted to bring an 18-year-old boy home with him the next day. She asked his name, and when David said Eldo she started crying. She asked, "David, is that the young boy who crawled over every person on the pew we were sitting on the night we heard the choir sing?" Continuing, she said, "He came directly to me and prayed for me. He gave me his bracelet with his name on it. I have been wearing it ever since... It's E – L – D – O, right?"

David was in tears, and his wife Lisa was in tears. With an obedient heart to the Lord, she said, "Bring him home." They bought an airline ticket for Eldo that night. That made it much easier for me to tell Eldo.

Eldo resides in Dawsonville, Ga with his amazing family and serves at his church. He is growing into an amazing young man because of the family God chose for him. Eldo came from what most people consider the most dangerous city in Haiti City Soleil. He is the recipient of multiple miracles from his surgery to the gift of this amazing family. Love Him Love Them is extremely grateful to the Allen's and all of our amazing host families for their commitment to our children and how they love him as if they were their own.

Eldo's new family from L-R David Allen, Fred Antoine, Gracey, Eldo, Lisa, Mirlanda, Mommy Linda and David

THE HUG GIRLS AND
THE TRANSITION HOME

CHAPTER TWENTY

Romans 15:13

*May the God of hope fill you with all joy and peace as you
trust in him, so that you may overflow with hope by the
power of the Holy Spirit.*

Having done mission work in Haiti for quite a few years now, I've had the opportunity to cross paths with many incredible ministries, and many fascinating people. One such ministry is Haiti Under God, who I'll hereafter refer to as HUG. Their ultimate mission is to change lives in Haiti through Jesus Christ. Introduced to Donald Lyons, the founder of HUG, and also to Bruce Williams, another member of HUG's Board of Directors, a few years ago, our shared passion for Haiti and Pastor Maxeau took center stage.

While HUG's ministry work had been primarily focused on a spectacularly beautiful, yet destitute mountaintop in Haiti called ChaCha Mountain, our ministry work has been focused at the base of that same mountaintop in the valley city of Galette Chambon, which we often refer to as the "Valley of Hope." Funnily enough, in order get

OPERATION CHRISTMAS CHILD ✛ GOOD NEWS. GREAT JOY.

Mommy Linda and Bruce Williams CEO of Haiti Under God (HUG) at Samaratins purse offices in Boone, NC just after meeting with SP Hospital division in hopes of securing funding for The Valley of Hope Hospital in Haiti

to ChaCha Mountain from the capital city of Port au Prince, Haiti, you have to drive through the Valley of Hope.

As the co-founder of the Love Him Love Them ministry with my husband David, one of my biggest frustrations in the world of ministry has been the seeming lack of partnership among many organizations with identical missions. I just think to myself how much more we could accomplish

(David and Linda Gunter (Co-founders of Love Him Love Them) Loretta and Donald Lyons (founder of Haiti Under God) and Pastor Maxeau (Founder of Valley of Hope))

if we broke down the barriers of an entrenched ministry and just worked together. Not to mention the Lord knows I need and I want all the help I can get!

Mommy Linda and Pastor Maxeau in Haiti showing off the concrete block maker purchased to use for training in The Valley of Hope Vocational School. In addition we have used it to make all of the blocks to build the hospital and the transition home. Upon completion of all building projects, we will open a concrete block store and sell the blocks to others

With the HUG ministry, that crossover of support began to develop naturally. With HUG having built a church and school on the top of ChaCha mountain, our mission teams would travel to that church and school every Christmas to deliver presents to the HUG communities. When HUG wanted to purchase a block maker for their many construction projects on the top of the mountain, we shared the cost so that same block maker could be used for construction projects in the valley. When HUG held an eye clinic for patients needing cataracts removed or vision support, we held a medical clinic alongside them. When HUG held a pastors' conference as part of their evangelism training, my husband David travelled to Haiti to lead a session. The list goes on and on. Needless to say, I'm grateful for the effortless partnership our ministries have forged over the years.

In 2018, during the middle of our third, and what we now know to be final, choir tour, Bruce Williams contacted me and said that Donald Lyons was stepping down from running Haiti Under God and that he, Bruce, would be the new CEO of HUG. He said their ministry's structure and focus was changing. They really wanted to focus on construction, agriculture and evangelism, and they wanted to mostly do this on ChaCha Mountain. At the time HUG was running an orphanage located close to the capital city of Port au Prince, and it just happened to be the second of the two orphanages we visited during our family's first mission trip to Haiti in 2011. It was an orphanage we continued to visit every year since that very first trip, watching the sweet young girls grow into beautiful young ladies, with every year that passed.

Bruce explained that, because the majority of their future trip participants to Haiti would be primarily men, they just didn't really see how it would work out to keep the all-girl's orphanage. He said that I was the first person he thought of to help with the girls because we had spent every Christmas with the girls since 2011. We loved the girls. However, I didn't really know the girls. What I did know was that we needed to find a solution for them. I left that phone call, after letting him know that I was interested in helping him find a solution, but that I needed to speak with my husband and our Board of Directors before making any commitments.

During that initial phone call, Bruce mentioned that five of their girls were turning 18, and they couldn't stay in the orphanage any longer. After talking with my husband David and our Board of Directors regarding Bruce's request that Love Him Love Them consider taking over the orphanage, I reached back out to Bruce to ask him what his plans or thoughts were for the five girls turning 18. He told me they had reached out to another organization, and that organization was putting together a proposal for the girls who would soon be too old to remain in the orphanage. Having known these girls since they were children, the idea of them leaving the orphanage with no home, no job, and no way to provide for themselves was an option none of us would even consider. With a conference call scheduled, Bruce wanted me to join in to get my input on the other organization's plans.

During our conference call, I came to learn that the organization Bruce had reached out to would help the girls aging out of the orphanage by starting a new program to house and educate girls who were 18 years old and older. To my dismay, they wanted a large amount of money to get the program up and running. Trying to wrap my mind around the funds requested, I politely thanked them for their time and went back to the drawing board to see what solution I could come up with for "our" girls, already accepting what the Lord had been orchestrating since our first visit to the HUG orphanage... that those girls would be ours to care for and ours to love.

With an idea formulated in my mind, I told David and Pastor Maxeau that, for the same amount of money being requested by the other organization, we could easily start our own program. With our five girls counting down the days for the Haitian government to demand their removal from their orphanage (with non- compliance risking the orphanage's certification), I was ready to dive into waters unknown to launch an official "Transition Home" program for orphaned girls who had reached the age of 18. We could launch the transition program immediately to care for our five oldest girls, and we'd have a ready solution for our many other girls coming through the orphanages. Both David and Pastor Maxeau agreed.

During my next phone call with Bruce, I let him know we were willing to take the girls, but we didn't want to move forward with funding another organization's transition program. With several other girls eventually coming through the program after our five 18-year-olds, we'd only be willing to fund our own program. Having worked on this idea for over a year, I'm not sure Bruce was completely thrilled, but we were ready to move forward.

Working through the details of taking on another orphanage, I again reached out to Bruce to ask him for the numbers. This included sponsorship numbers and numbers on however else they were supporting the girls. Most of their funding came from a boarding house for mission travelers, aptly named My Father's Guest House. So, I naturally proceeded to ask, "If we are going to take on the liability and the expense of caring for the girls, isn't it only logical that you would also give us the asset of the guesthouse?" Bruce said he would have to ask his Board of Directors about that.

The series of phone calls that followed consisted of negotiations for the guest house. These negotiations were all being managed in between choir concerts, traveling, and caring for our other orphanage of kids temporarily residing in the United States, not an easy feat. While at first we were considering paying for the guest house, after several calls, we found that they were giving the guest house to us. All the agreements were made, and effective July 1, 2018, Love Him

Love Them took over the responsibility of funding and running the HUG orphanage of 17 girls, at which time we were transferred the "asset" of My Fathers Guest House. I was very excited about the Guest House, as it had only been rented out at about 25% capacity. I knew we could increase that booking volume, which would help with not only funding the girls, but would fund several other projects we had in Haiti!

My Fathers Guest House Delmas Haiti

Phyllis Van Es and a few members of the amazing staff at My Father's Guest House in Haiti. Come stay with us www.MyFathersGuestHouse.com

Two days after being handed the keys to the HUG orphanage and My Father's Guest House, civil unrest hit in Haiti, and it reached an extreme we had never seen before. All reservations at the guest house for the rest of 2018 were cancelled. No one was traveling to Haiti. One political event after another led to an almost endless cycle of riots, gang activity, and manifestations in the streets of Haiti, and most mission group that had previously visited Haiti on an annual basis and those that had pre-booked a trip to Haiti in 2019 either cancelled, or never re-booked.

As we said good-bye to 2019 and welcomed in 2020 with a new spring in our step, I'm sure I don't need to tell you what happened. The Covid-19 global pandemic of 2020 hit, and again we were left without guests. I jokingly like to claim that, if I didn't know any better, I would think somehow Bruce and the HUG Board of Directors had some kind of "insider information." The timing was just unbelievable, truly unbelievable!

With the continuing uncertainty, our Board of Directors discussed the fate of our guest house on multiple occasions. But the decision was always made, that when God was ready for us to shut it down, we'd know. As long as we had money available in the bank account to pay for the guest house, we'd keep it up and running. No math could possibly explain our ability to pay the rent on the building housing My Father's Guest House with NO guests. Considering our additional monthly expenses, including salaries for the staff of ten, food for the staff, electricity, city water, vehicle upkeep and care, and diesel fuel for the generators, it is truly astounding how we were able to keep the doors open. And yet, as I write this in 2021, the guest house is still open. The staff is all still in place, and we are patiently awaiting visitors to return to Haiti. God's math is not the same as ours!

On top of keeping the guest house doors open, 2019 and 2020 brought many new changes for the HUG orphanage girls. Deciding to stop the lease on the home where the girls had previously been living, we moved the girls who were under the age of 18 to a treasured orphanage run by Pastor Maxeau and his family called Hope and Love. We opened a vocational school for young women who needed continuing education in practical and employable skills, such as sewing, cooking, cosmetology, and the like. Here, our girls who had aged out of the orphanage, unable to afford a college education and not yet ready or able to find work in Haiti, had a program available to them to continue their training.

Very 1st Valley of Hope Vocational School Graduation

(L to R) Lauren Lee, Bonnie Fields and Charlene Lee at very first Vocational School Graduation. These ladies provided amazing gifts to each student to get them set up in their new careers. Cosmetology, Cooking, Construction, Computers, Crafts (Beauty for Ashes Jewelry Business), Concrete Block Making and Sewing.

Key administration in Haiti at the 1st Valley of Hope Vocational School Graduation

Our dream had always been to add a second story to our vocational school, to serve as a transition home for all of our girls as they aged out of the orphanages. In 2018, we were excited to learn that a church had stepped up to commit the funds for beginning the addition to the school, but they sadly had to back out, to our great disappointment. With some creative reorganizing, we transformed four rooms of the vocational school into a dormitory for our girls who had aged out of the orphanage. With one room serving as a kitchen, one as a living room, one as a bedroom with bunk beds, and the last for the administrator, or overseer, of the transition home, the girls had a special place to call home.

Planning for the future, knowing it wouldn't be long before the current set of transitioning girls finished their vocational training, and were ready for employment and newfound independence, we purchased land to build 100 homes within walking distance of the Vocational School. For the girls who chose to seek employment within our community, they could build a home and still remain geographically close to their network of support.

1st home under construction in The Valley of Hope Neighborhood in Haiti

1st home completed in 2021 in The Valley of Hope Neighborhood in Haiti

In the last week of 2020, I received an email that said the following:

"Hi Linda, it's Ginger.

I went on the 2017 Teachers Teaching Teachers How to Teach mission trip, and my heart has been burdened for those girls who need a Transition Home. I have actually been upset with God for laying this continually on my heart, because I am a school teacher and a mom of 6 kids, and I do not have the means to build them a home. I wanted to check with you to see if you were still looking for a way to complete this project and if so, how much it would cost."

I responded immediately to let her know it was definitely still a need, and I let her know the cost to finish the project which was a very large amount. Ginger said that was much more than they had ever anticipated. She explained that her mother-in-law had passed away and that prior to her death, she had been squirreling away money that no one knew about. Ginger said her family would need to discuss this amount, which was much larger than they had anticipated, and would get back to me.

Ginger called me the next morning and said that she and her family felt God was seeing how faithful they would be, and she said that they decided that, even though this project was bigger than anything they could have anticipated, they served a God that was bigger than the project funds. To my overwhelming and unparalleled joy, they wanted to move forward.

Ginger and her beautiful family responsible for the Transition Home in Haiti being completed

So, in the year of 2020, in the middle of a global pandemic, from out of nowhere the funds arrived for us to complete the final stages of our Transition Home project. For those of you calculating, that is 17 months after we accepted all 17 girls into our hearts. As I write to you now, we have just had our first two girls transition out of the home, and five more will soon move into the home. All of the girls are still in school, each of them has found employment – either working at the hospital, the school or the church, or for the Beauty for Ashes Jewelry Line

Once again, God has provided more than we could have ever thought of, hoped for, or imagined!!!

Transition Home building in progress in 2020

Transition home in June 2021
Scheduled to open Dec 1. 2021

GIRLS' CHOIR VISAS
TURNED DOWN TWICE / COVID

CHAPTER TWENTY ONE

The close of our 2018 Haitian Orphan Choir tour marked three seasons on the road with Magine, Micheline, Belinda, Mirlanda, Samaika, Seyma, Eldo, Davidson, and the other children from their orphanage in Haiti. With most children now settled in the United States with loving host families and the opportunity of schooling, we as a ministry felt it was time to give another group of orphans the opportunity to experience the wonder and gift of travel to the United States for the following year's choir tour. However, with a new group of orphans came the arduous process of obtaining the performance visas for the kids needed in order to tour in the United States.

For those of you not familiar with the process, to get a plane ticket you must have a visa, to get a visa you have to have a passport, to get a passport you have to have a birth certificate, and to have a birth certificate you have to know your birthday. With most of the orphans in Haiti having lost their families in the devastating 2010 earthquake, I was starting at ground zero. In each case, the child is frequently the only survivor found in the ruins and rubble, and there is no one to ask about their birthdate. Furthermore, any records in Haiti were either destroyed by the earthquake or corrupt government officials, so going to a local government office to retrieve information wasn't an easy solution either.

With the girls from both Pastor Maxeau's Hope and Love Orphanage and our Transition Home, 2019 was going to be the debut of the Haitian Orphan Girls' Choir in America. This meant we had to begin the arduous visa process again, this time on behalf of thirty-three girls, ages 5 to 22 -- and so we did. The paperwork seems to take forever. This is one of my very least favorite things in the entire world to do, not just this paperwork but any paperwork! We put everything together and sent it off to the U.S. Homeland Security department. We had a set of interns in Haiti -- Haley and Emilee -- to work with the girls before their departure to the United States. Our interns taught the girls English and customs in America.

We waited with much anticipation, and then, in June 2019, our response to the visa applications arrived. The choir was not "culturally unique" enough, and their visa application was denied. Our girls in Haiti were so eager anticipating this choir tour -- not only because coming to America to sing would be the thrill of a lifetime, but also because they each had the dream that they, too, might find loving families and be able to attend school in the U.S.

Haitian ALL GIRLS CHOIR ready to come to United States but visas denied in 2019 and 2020

Reginald, Choir and Music Director. Beautiful girls from our Hope and Love orphanage in Haiti and The Transition Home. These are the girls who made up the Love Him Love Them Haitian Girls choir whose visas were denied in both 2019 and 2020. Their voices sound like angels. You should order their CD!

With the girls' dreams and expectations so very high, I couldn't understand God's reasoning for not paving the way for the girls to come. We were so confident that the tour would happen, we had already booked the majority of our concert locations. We already had the costumes made, and housing lined up. We already had interns waiting in Haiti with the children, planning to spend their entire summer on tour with the choir. One of those interns, Emilee, was planning to have the girls sing at her wedding, which had been scheduled with the choir tour in mind. We were all devastated. Unable to delay the news that the tour was not going to happen that year, our intern Haley, along with our ministry board member, Doug, were burdened with the task of sharing the disappointing news with our girls, who were waiting expectantly in Haiti. Doug later shared with me how difficult and disturbing it was to see these girls – who had been filled with so much hope -- fall so quickly into despair.

During this time, I was faced with anther struggle, another source of discouragement. Two of the children from our previous choir tours, 15-year-old Ibendo and 8-year-old Mirlanda, no longer had host families willing to keep and care for them. For lack of a better term, they were returned to us. With Mirlanda having faced rejection so many times, my husband David moved her into our home with the intent to keep her, to give her some stability. And not yet having a placement for Ibendo, he also moved into our home until we could determine the best path forward.

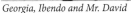
Georgia, Ibendo and Mr. David

(Several weeks after Mirlanda moved into our home Mommy Linda and Mirlanda on the plane to Haiti for a trip to the Embassy to redo paperwork to allow her to stay in the united States.)

In the face of upheaval and uncertainty, and in the midst of despair, my mind was flooded with questions. "Is it over? Are we done? How will we go forward from here? What is the new plan? How can we possibly raise the funds to continue? What will we do? How will we do it? Should we just quit? What am I going to do with the kids? Is God protecting us? Is God teaching us a lesson? What do we do now? Do we try again?" Questioning and overwhelmed, I received a final big blow.

Macarena, my best friend for many, many years, and "the oil" that made the choir tour run, came to my home and told me she was moving to Texas and would no longer be able to work for the ministry. Her sister had made her an offer she couldn't refuse, and she was leaving in 30 days. I had no idea how to do what Macarena did, day-in and day-out, at the Love Him Love Them office. And after the shock of the devastating news wore off, I decided it didn't really matter because, without the choir tour and without Macarena, I might as well just shut everything down. I felt certain with everything falling apart, this was surely a "sign" that it was time quit.

The only thread keeping me tethered to the ministry was my husband, David. He did not share my feelings about this being a sign, and he wasn't willing to concede defeat. With time, he talked me out of the despair. He was my source of reason when my deceitful heart

Macarena and my family serving at one of THE MANY Love Him Love Them events L to R Front Row Carrie Second Row Cameron, Macarena, Jazzy, Daleesha, Mommy Linda, Mr. David)

Mommy Linda and Mommy Macarena

could only see betrayal. Time went on, and we somehow kept the ministry moving forward. The next ministry event we focused on was preparing and delivering Thanksgiving dinner to thousands of people in need, and it was amazing! We stepped up our game that year, as we have every year since then, adding multiple sponsors, volunteer t-shirts, and a Feed the Hunger event, where volunteers packed meals of rice and beans to send down to our communities in Haiti.

In 2020, we went through the entire Visa application process again for the Haitian orphan girls' choir, and we were once again denied. In retrospect, I cannot imagine what would have happened if we had brought those girls to the United States in 2020 when the Covid pandemic was in full swing, travel was restricted, and churches were shut down. And yet, after two years with NO CHOIR TOUR -- , the primary source of our fundraising in the three previous years -- something TRULY UNBELIEVABLE happened. In the middle of a global pandemic, we opened our hospital in Haiti – and not only that, we received funding to complete our Transition Home! Who would have thought? I certainly couldn't have conceived of these victories just one short year earlier. It was more than we could have ever hoped for or imagined!

Valley of Hope Hospital under construction

OPEN HOSPITAL IN MIDDLE OF GLOBAL PANDEMIC

CHAPTER TWENTY TWO

Romans 8:28

And we know that in all things God works for the good of those who love him, who have been called according to his purpose.

One day in 2016, a lady in the final stages of labor arrived on the back of a moto bike taxi in Galette Chambon, Haiti – eighteen miles east of Port-au-Prince. Here, you can find our Valley of Hope community. The tap-tap driver brought the lady down from one of the nearby mountains on what was a very long drive. The woman's screams from her pain caused him to pull the moto bike into the center of our Valley of Hope. Seeing buildings, he assumed there would be medical help available there. Instead of a medical center, however, they found a school and church. Not able to make it any further, the people in the community helped as best they could, but they had no medical training. Sadly, both the mother and her baby died. When I learned of this horrible tragedy, the first words out of my mouth were, "We have to build and open a hospital in Haiti!"

Two years passed, and on February 2, 2018, our handsome 10-year-old orphaned boy, Sonsay, passed away in Haiti from Typhoid Fever. Compounding the tragedy was the fact that Typhoid is an easily treatable disease when patients have access to basic healthcare and commonly available medication. We now had two reasons to open a hospital. With the funds raised during our 2018 choir tour, "Sonsay's Season," we raised enough funds to begin construction of the hospital.

Over the next 18 months, construction moved forward. Although we were planning to have an influx of donors in 2019 while touring with our all-girls' Haitian Orphan Choir, no visas meant no choir tour. Despite the setback, construction on the hospital proceeded forward. As donations earmarked for the hospital were received, they were sent down to Haiti to fund the next stage of the building project.

As 2020 approached, we had made a lot of headway on the construction project. However, we needed another big push for additional funding to complete this ambitious project. We set forth plans to host a huge fundraising gala in March 2020 to raise the remaining funds needed to finish construction and open the hospital. Sadly, our plans came to an abrupt end because of the pandemic. Two days before the scheduled date of the event, the United States began to impose serious stay-at-home orders, and live concerts of any kind were no longer a possibility. With great heaviness of heart, we were forced to cancel our gala.

As the seriousness of the global pandemic escalated, our ministry knew that now, more than ever, the Haitian people living in the area around the hospital were in great need of medical care and attention. We could only imagine the devastation that would occur if Covid ran rampantly through the country of Haiti. As Covid continued to close doors, we, as a ministry, continued to pray behind those closed doors. The Lord revealed that we could pivot and open as a medical clinic. But beyond that, we had no idea what to do or how to do it. And then, like a bright shining light in the darkness, the exact amount of funding we needed to open the clinic trickled in! There was, literally, no explanation for the way this much needed money materialized. No single donor came to our rescue, and we didn't ask anyone for anything. Well, that's not completely true. We did ask God for help!

On August 29, 2020, in the middle of a global pandemic, we opened the first level of our hospital as a medical clinic. We planned for the hospital to only be open limited hours, from 8am until to 3pm, daily. I had the privilege of traveling to Haiti to join in the amazing celebration of the hospital's grand opening. It was a gift to be able to stand in front of the hospital and welcome in the community. In honor of our grand opening, all medical services were provided free of charge. The hope this building brought to the community was tangible.

Mommy Linda, Mommy Anne and Pastor Maxeau at Ribbon Cutting Grand Opening of Hospital August 29, 2020

Architects drawing for completed Hospital

The Valley of Hope Hospital August 2020 Waiting for God to provide to finish!

On the first day we were open, forty minutes before closing time, a young woman in labor came waddling into the hospital. She was placed in a room with me, and the hospital's head doctor asked me to monitor the young woman. Forty minutes later, we had our very first baby born at The Love Him Love Them Valley of Hope Hospital in Haiti -- an amazing gift! I truly felt like it was God's sign of approval, or even almost a "thank you" gift, for remaining dedicated to the Lord's purpose during a season when fear prevailed. I can't fully describe the realization that, the very spot where a pregnant mother died giving birth only four years earlier was now the site of a new hospital where a new mother celebrated the joyous birth of her new baby. I was in awe of the Lord, humbled that he would allow me to witness the culmination

of his good and perfect plan.

First baby born in hospital on Opening Day)

Mommy Linda and first baby born in Valley if Hope Hospital on opening Day

Dr. Roberdo, Nurse, Mommy Ann and Mommy Linda with first baby born at Valey of Hope Hospital on Opening Day

Needless to say, we did not close at 3pm on that first day, as we had originally planned. The next day, with another new mother welcoming twins into the world from another hospital bed, we didn't make our 3pm closing either. As a matter of fact, the hospital's doors have remained open ever since!

(Twins born on Day 2 of The Valley of Hope Hospital being open. This mother had no idea she was carrying twins)

JODY BENNETT
AND WONDERING WHY

CHAPTER TWENTY THREE

Romans 8:28

And we know that in all things God works for the good of those who love him, who have been called according to his purpose.

Each night on the choir tour was an adventure. Most times, when we pulled into a church, we never REALLY knew if we were at the right place. By the third year, we would ask as nicely as we could for the churches to put us on their outside sign or marquee. Funnily enough, it was not only to advertise that we would be there. It was mainly so when we pulled into the parking lot, we would know we were at the right place.

One time, we were following GPS enroute to a church in Madison, Georgia, and we arrived a little early. We pulled up to the front door to unload, and as we started to take the musical instruments inside, we saw a sign on the front door that said, "NO GUNS OR FIREARMS ALLOWED." We chuckled and then headed on inside to get set up. Back outside, unloading more of the instruments, we saw someone coming from inside the church, heading to meet us at the front door. I went to introduce myself, and he said, "Now why are ya'll bringing in these instruments? We don't know nuthin' about no choir here today. Let me make a call." In the meantime, I checked our tour schedule and called our contact listed for the church where we were scheduled to sing, and yes, you guessed it. We were at the wrong church. I'm busting up laughing as I remember this. I really don't know what was the funniest, the sign? Unloading and setting up in a place we weren't supposed to be? Or the fact that we just walked into the church.

Another time we were scheduled to sing at a place called "Unity on a Mission" in Hoschton, Georgia. When we pulled up, I was totally convinced we were at the wrong place, because it was a house – a regular house, where a family might live, with a garage door and everything. There was barely enough room for me to get the bus down the driveway. We got out to see how far away we were from the right place, and it ended up we were at the right place. The house was the headquarters of a trucking company that had a group of people who met in a little garage just under the office for praise and worship. When we unloaded, there were more of us in the choir than there were room for people in the audience. During the entirety of my performance, I just kept thinking to myself, "What in the world are we doing here?"

Fast forward four years, and we were shipping a container full of medical supplies to Haiti to use in the hospital we opened. We needed a truck and a driver to get the 40' container to the port in Miami. It was going to cost $2,500 just for transport down to Miami, not to mention the container fees, ocean transport fees, and customs fees. We were at the office seeking God's guidance, and Lisa, who works in our office, said, "Linda, do you remember telling that story about when you sang at that garage. It was the one owned by a trucking company, and you never knew why you were there. What if we called and asked them to help us?" Lisa made the call and explained what we were looking for. Jody Bennett, who ran the trucking company said, "Absolutely, we remember the choir. We were just sitting here wondering how we could serve your ministry. Shipping containers is what we do every day. Of course, we would love to help you, and we are happy to pay for it!" We have since packed and shipped two containers to Haiti and will soon ship a third. Jody has not only helped with the containers but has also provided numerous volunteers for events and has become a dear friend.

It is always humbling when you get to see the other side of God's plans and can trace back how he has orchestrated the things in our lives that we never could have hoped for or imagined. It seemed so ridiculous to me at the time when we sang in that little garage under that trucking company's office. But of course, little did I know what God had in store.

First container Love Him Love Them shipped to Haiti

Volunteers packing 3rd Container shipped by Love Him Love Them to Haiti. This one is full of Earthquake relief supplies shipped September 2021

These students from Haiti (pictured with our favorite Truck Driver Willie) currently in The United States on student visas helped pack this container full of earthquake relief supplies to go to Haiti after the August 14, 2021 magnitude 7.2 eathquake (L to R) Brice, Fred, Mirlanda, Samaika, Belinda, Willie, Samuel and Redphca

(Jody Bennett and Mommy Linda just before entering studio to share on WGGS- TV's Nite Line about shipping a container to Haiti full of much needed supplies)

FINAL THOUGHTS

CHAPTER TWENTY FOUR

My journey in ministry over the past few years has not been without immense challenge. Without the pit of despair and heartbreak, we may never have the opportunity to appreciate that God is the light in the darkness. We only need to Trust Him, moment by moment. When things are dark and bleak, we trust him. When things are going well, we trust Him. We trust Him when things are going well. This type of trust requires no exertion of our will. When things go wrong, we are faced with the choice of intentionally trusting or rebelling. We must choose to trust in all circumstances.

Because of all these things that happened, we had to search what the truth was we had to find the truth and we had to live out that truth.

As I send this book off to the publishers in July of 2021, tension in Haiti is at an all-time high. The number of kidnapping incidents has increased, and there is dangerous political instability. The remarkable volunteers of our Love Him Love Them ministry remain undaunted; however, I believe that the future is bright. I invite you to join us in this life affirming mission, one that brings joy and hope to orphans of Haiti each day. We recently had our annual Volunteer Extravaganza and I want you to know about just a few people who shared at that event.

14 year old Halllie Ferguson who has volunteered at all of our Thanksgiving events in America where we deliver food and so much more to Hopeless, Homeless and Homebound individuals shared about how she encouraged her school club to raise funds to help with Christmas Joy bags for Haiti. She and her club did several fund-raising

events in 2020 and helped with almost $2,000.00. These were 7th and 8th graders.

Hallie and her amazing family!

Danny Yearwood, the chaplain of the Stephens County Jail shared about the reactions of the inmates when they saw the images and videos of their children receiving Christmas gifts at our "Night of Hope" annual event held in Northeast Georgia. He had to choke back the tears as he shared about volunteering at the event and seeing the children and spouses and families of the inmates he was working with on the inside. He said there was no way for us to realize the impact this made on the inmates to know that in a small way they were able to participate in their children's Christmas.

Bethany Stratton, mother of 3 and the Love Him Love Them Vacation Bible School creator / Director and Developer shared about the 2nd VBS program that she and her group of Volunteers have put

Danny Yearwood, My friend and Chaplain of Stephens County Jail

together that is available on our www.LoveHImlovethem.org website. She shared about how children around the world can now learn about life in Haiti including the cultural snacks, crafts and videos of all we participate in Haiti. What an opportunity for children's directors and VBS Directors to have this program available to them FREE to use wether as an entire VBS program or a Summer once a week program or even as an add on for the Missions portion to attach to a VBS you are already using. Bethany shared how remarkable churches thought

it was to not only learn about the children in the country but then to be able to have the Haitian Orphan children's choir come to their church to share at the end of VBS in person really brought the Mission program to life.

(Bethany Stratton receiving The Love Him Love Them Volunteer of the year award for 2018 from David Gunter, co-founder of Love Him Love Them)

Irene Jackson, 70 years old received The Volunteer of the Year award at the event. She shared about importance of the Love Him Love Them family and how you can't do life alone. Irene shared about how some of the core volunteers of Love Him Love Them rallied around her the year prior when her husband Tom passed away. Irene was brought to tears sharing about how she volunteers in all aspects of the ministry and how there are opportunities for everyone.

Emilee Farnum, a newlywed and brand-new mom to newborn MK shared about her experience in Haiti as an intern. She brought to life for everyone in the room who had never been to Haiti many of her experiences with the girls we all know and love who call the

Transition Home their home. Emilee is our Volunteer Mission Trip Coordinator, and she shared her disappointment with the current situation in Haiti not allowing our trips to continue as planned currently. Emilee cried uncontrollably as she asked everyone in the room to please pray for the protection of all our children and staff in Haiti.

Emilee in Haiti during her internship with Love Him Love Them

Lisa Lafleur shared about our Sponsorship Program. She and several volunteers head up this amazing portion of Love Him Love Them and keep the children's sponsors updated with what is happening in their lives. She told us we have a vibrant program allowing children and sponsors the ability to communicate. She shared about the amazing Teachers and Pastors sponsor program and told about how awesome it is to have a church reach out to help a pastor in Haiti and and to also have American Teachers sponsor teachers in Haiti who teach the same subjects as

Lisa Lafleur Welshman Executive Director of Love Him Love Them and Pastor Maxeau

they do. Lisa became emotional as she shared about all of the progress of the donations and help coming for the newly opened hospital in Haiti and is excited to see who the donor will be to finish the top 2 levels of construction.

Phyllis Van Es joined the Extravaganza via zoom from MyFathersGuestHouse.com in Haiti. Phyllis is our American Volunteer Guest House Director in Haiti. She was teaching her Gospel English class in Haiti and very excited to let her Haitian students practice their English by allowing them to introduce themselves to us. There was limited Wi-Fi and a scratchy connection, but 69-year-old Phyllis was as energetic as always to share with everyone and give us updates of the shootings and civil unrest in Haiti.

Wesley Farnum, the amazing husband of Emilee and daddy of MK and owner of Waypoint Marketing (Waypointmkt.com) a Digital Marketing firm is our Volunteer Website Designer. He shared about he and his wife's trips to Haiti and how they impacted their lives forever. He stressed that he and Emilee had been volunteering for several years and as newlyweds and new parents and they did not intend to stop. Wesley and Emilee live over 3 hours away from our headquarters in NE Georgia but are 100% involved in the day to day operations.

I had the honor of officiating Wesley and Emilee's wedding ceremony. We went through 16 weeks of pre-marital counseling. I love them both so much! Here we are walking down the aisle about to wait for Emilee's grand entrance!

Susan Blakely, Linda's Volunteer Assistant shared about all she is involved with on a day-to-day basis and the excitement level of being in the midst of everything happening with Love Him Love Them. Susan shared through tears about how her life has changed since working so closely with Linda and how she is constantly amazed at all we are doing both in the United States and in Haiti. She stressed how we need help in so many areas and talked about the Beauty for Ashes jewelry ministry that employs almost 200 women in Haiti from making jewelry out of recycled trash.

Susan Blakely, Volunteer Assistant to Mommy Linda

Kim Steckelberg showed off the beautiful new designs from the

LOVE LINE of custom-made necklaces from the Beauty from Ashes Jewelry Line. She told about the incredible uniqueness of each handmade bead and how incredible it was to know that each lady in Haiti working with the jewelry business was able to provide for her family. She asked that everyone keep their eyes open for boutiques to potentially promote the necklaces, earrings and bracelets made by the ladies in Haiti and directed everyone in attendance to the www.

Kim Steckelberg and Mommy Linda

LoveHimLoveThem.org website to purchase the gorgeous one of a kind jewelry. We are blessed to have Shirley Phillips who is a great model for the jewelry line and great at running the product table at our events.

Front Row: Mirlanda, Caden, SHIRLEY PHILLIPS

Back Row: David Gunter, Jeanna Merilien, Fred, Mommy Linda

Doug and Debbie Vermilya received a ceremonial key at the event to commemorate their donation to build the first home in the Love Him Love Them Neighborhood in Haiti. It was also Debbie's birthday, and she was brought to tears when the picture of the home was displayed.

Pastor Maxeau from Haiti also joined us virtually. He shared about the civil unrest and how grateful he was for Love Him Love Them and how we work together to change the lives of so many people in Haiti. He thanked everyone at the event for the continued support and asked for everyone to pray for the safety of all the Valley of Hope administration in Haiti.

Pastor Maxeau Antoine, the man with the vision, the founder of The Valley of Hope Ministry in Haiti

Pastor Maxeau and his wife Mommy Anne and their family Alicia, Samuel, Chloe and Fred

You cannot medicate a spiritual problem…….

Everything I have shared with you in this book (and trust me I only scratched the surface of the occurrences of a 3-year time frame) happens every day in each one of your lives. You or someone you know may not have levitated in the air or ran through a vehicle and survived or had the voice of Satan speak out of their mouth. However, you or someone you know have been depressed, anxious, worried, or even just felt out of your mind at some point and maybe even right now. My whole purpose for sharing the outlandish experiences I had in this book is to help you realize that you and I have an enemy. Satan and his demons look to destroy the work of God and deceive anyone they can (1Peter 5:8, 2 Corinthians 11:14-15) Satan and his demons deceive the world (2 Corinthians 4:4) and spread false doctrine (1 Timothy 4:1) attack Christians (2 Corinthians 12:7) and combat the Holy angels. These demons are described as evil spirits (Matthew 10:1) lying spirits (1Kings 22:23) . They are the voices full of lies that told our girls to strangle themselves and to kill themselves and they are the same lying voices that tell you that you are worthless and no good and that you don't measure up and that you are an outcast. WE HAVE TO KNOW THE TRUTH. The fact that I read the Bible my entire life and did Bible study after Bible study and still was completely unprepared to fight off the demonic realm that I came face to face with is disheartening at best. It just makes me downright mad. It breaks my heart that Christian women just like me who are yearning to be close to God and raise their families to love Jesus and be the wife God wants them to can be so deceived. Satan deceived Eve with food in the beginning and he is still deceiving us with food and many other things. He knows exactly where to shoot his fiery darts.

Without our shield of FAITH in place the darts make it right through. Our faith must be in Jesus and the TRUTH he has taught us and the knowledge that the same power resides in us that Jesus used to raise Lazarus from the dead. Without faith it is impossible to please God (Hebrew 11:6). We say we have faith but our actions and the way we live our lives speak otherwise. Matthew 6:34 The Bible tells us do not worry and do not be anxious (Philippians 4:6 and 7) and yet people who profess to be Christians almost brag about worrying and being anxious. I hear people who profess to be Christians literally bragging about their anti-anxiety medicine they take and how it doesn't work so they add another one. "Fear not" is in the Bible over 365 times. I'm pretty sure that means we are not to fear. Fear is FAITH in Satan. If you had the opportunity to sit down and speak with any of our girls that experienced these horrible experiences, they would share with you once we were able to drill down with them that they were scared. They were experiencing fear. If you talk to Samaika now, she will tell you she hears the same voice NOW, telling her to do the same thing that before ended her up on the floor rolling around like a crazy person and now she speaks back to the voice out loud and says "I am not scared of you I am a child of God, get away from me you have no right to speak to me in the name of Jesus GO!" She has NO FEAR now. That is one of the biggest keys. You need to figure out what you are afraid of what is the fear? There are so many things to fear but God has promised us He will never leave us He will never forsake us. Ultimately, if we really BELIEVE what Jesus tells us in the Bible we do not have any reason to fear anything.

But for some reason in the United States, we don't typically see what we saw in Haiti. Now, if you have spent any length of time in a

3rd world country the demonic realm is very obvious. If you look at the picture of Jeremy, the prior voodoo priest it isn't hard to recognize the evil he is doing when he has on his mask and is conjuring up voodoo. But in America, we are so easily deceived by the music, movies, television, social media, pornography, or a group of women gossiping at a coffee shop. Satan and his demons really do not have to work too hard in the United States because most of us are partnering with the demonic realm and don't even seem to realize it. We allow our children to watch Disney movies with homosexual characters and fairy's and magic spells and that use God's name as a curse word. Our kids listen to music that is so demonic we don't even know what the words say. Our spouses and children spend more time on social media looking at who knows what than at any Family Dinner table or in any Family conversation. We take our children to Harry Potter movies and buy them toys with zombies to play with. We dress our children up and make Satan laugh as we change their identity on Halloween, one of the most evil and Satanic holidays of the year. (Jude 3-4) It is just as if we are completely deceived and are in no way compelled to fight strenuously for the defense of the faith. It is as if certain people have crept in unnoticed just as if they were sneaking in a side door. They are ungodly persons who distort the grace of God into decadence and immoral freedom viewing it as an opportunity to do whatever they want and deny or disown our only Master and Lord Jesus Christ.

When Tony the Tiger is leading the gay pride parade and we do not have the fervency to fast and pray for Kellogg, somewhere we have mixed up the line between compassion for the lost and our Faith in Jesus Christ. (Jude 7)

We are warned over and over about the demonic realm. We have been told our battle is not against another person but against a very organized and strategic group of principalities. WE ARE ALL IN A BATTLE. That part is not an option. The choice we do have is whether or not we are going to fight. The only way to fight and win is to know our opponent and their strategies, (Just like in sports, coaches and players spend hours learning how their opponents play the game) We have to do the same if we want to win. Satan's job is to destroy us while we are here and rob us of our joy and get us medicated up and have us unhealthy and ruin our marriages and steal our children from us. Our job is to destroy the works of Satan and live an abundant life WHILE WE ARE HERE. It is possible. I am living proof. We can live above our circumstances. We can want to give up but not. We can have faith. We can believe. We can not worry. We can see miraculous healings! We can cast out demons. We can raise the dead. We can truly use the dunamis power (DYNOMITE) that God has placed inside of us and change lives. Don't waste another day of your life. Don't wait until crows turn into people and kids start levitating and Satan is speaking out of people's mouths. STOP right now and completely surrender your life, ask God to baptize you 100% in the Holy spirit, baptize is just being fully emersed in something. Listen to the Holy spirit, be obedient when He tells you to do or not to do something. Know the Word of God, hide it in your heart, meditate on it. You must know the word, so you know the Truth, so you know when the demonic voices come to you know it is NOT true. Do not try to medicate a spiritual problem. Healing is available. Forgive. Unforgiveness is a blockage to healing, right here, right now if you have someone you need to forgive DO IT. Stop worshiping Satan by continuing to hold bitterness, rage and anger and unforgiveness toward that person. TODAY is the day, right now is the moment to forgive. Offense is the bait of Satan he uses it to grab you and once you are offended it easily turns into unforgiveness and bitterness. JUST REFUSE it! Let Satan know this is his last opportunity to get you offended about anything tell him now "Don't worry, it will never happen again!"

ADDENDUM:
ON THE 17TH DAY OF THE SEVENTH MONTH

I shared with you in the beginning of this book that I received my 5 children on the 17th day of the 7th month of the year 2007 and it brought our family to the size of seven with children the ages of 7 to 17. People sometimes look at me funny when I go to the effort to explain all these numbers. In the beginning I thought it just happened that way so I could remember it. However, I have since learned the following. I truly believe now that God has ordained things in our lives. I do not believe God had anything to do with my friend's husband murdering her. I believe God is in charge. Not in control. The same way I "was in charge" of the bus, but everyone on that bus had free will and could choose what to do. After learning the following from the Word of God I believe the 17th day of the 7th month really does mean something to God. Just listen.....

Careful note was given to explain that Noah's Ark landed on Ararat on "the seventeenth day of the seventh month" (Genesis 8:4). After remaining in the grave for three days Christ rose from the dead on the 17th. . Christ, our Passover (I Corinthians 5:7), was slain on that day, but then rose three days later, on the seventeenth day of the seventh month of the civil calendar" The 17th day of the 7th month is the 17th of Nisan on the Jewish Calendar, and this corresponds to our April 17th. It appears that there is more to this day than the above mentioned. Indeed, deliverance first came on the 17th of Nisan through the Ark of Noah. However, a second deliverance came on the same day (17th of Nisan) years later at the parting of the Red Sea.

" (Joshua 5:13). Joshua then received detailed instructions of how to conquer Jericho. Jericho itself did not fall until seven days later due to the seven days of marching around the city walls but one can say that the same day the angel gave Joshua those instructions was the same day in which Jericho and the promised land was delivered into Israelite hands.

(Esther 5:1) Esther went to the king and invited he and Haman to a banquet the following day; the 17th of Nisan. It was at this banquet that Haman's evil tricks were exposed, and he was executed by the king while at the same time the Jews once again had been delivered.

As mentioned at the beginning of this section by far the most important of all the events that took place on the 17th of Nisan was the resurrection of Christ. A seventh deliverance, but for all mankind. As you know Christ was crucified on the 14th of Nisan, the day the Passover began. After remaining in the grave for three days Christ rose from the dead on the 17th

If one calculates the odds of so many important events occurring on any given day you come up with 1 in 783,864,876,960,000,000 chances that such events could take place. From this alone it is clear that God controls the world, and He watches over His people. Isn't it wonderful to have a personal relationship with such a loving and powerful God who has promised heavenly dwellings for all who follow Him. Certainly, nothing stands in the way of this promise, not even Satan himself.

(As of the publication of this book in late 2021 Linda is currently touring with 5 girls who were originally members of The Haitian Orphan Children's Choir. They are pictured below. Please reach out to Linda at 706-599-7525 or Linda @ LoveHimLoveThem.org for speaking opportunities)

(L to R, Redaphca, Thaina, Samaika, Mirlanda, Andremise, Belinda and Mommy Linda)

(Love Him Love Them Board of Directors 2021 L-R Kelly Breymeier. Doug Vermilya, Michael Keith, Bill Thomas, David Gunter, Linda Gunter)

There are no words to describe my gratitude to this godly group. Without them I would be nothing. They are my rock, foundation, prayer partners, guides, and a pure gift from God. It is an honor to work side by side with these who have my back, front side, and cover me constantly. The wisdom in this picture is hidden by shorts and tennis shoes. I love each of you more than you could possibly imagine. Thank you for letting me cry and be transparent and crazy and still loving me.

(Love Him Love Them Home Group meets every Sunday Night for Dinner and Bible Study)

A FEW FINAL THANK YOU'S

Greg Perkins CEO of African American Expressions,
Barbara Schuler (Linda's mom) Mommy Linda and Jackie

Give the Gift of Love!

Love Him Love Them is a nonprofit organization that exists to help widows and orphans in distress by meeting their spiritual, economic and physical needs through salvation, housing, occupations, education and sustenance. On the first trip to Haiti that Love Him Love Them went on, what they saw, smelled and experienced completely wrecked them. They knew something had to be done. The work in Haiti will never stop, but we can continue to make progress through our many projects including churches, schools, orphan care, hospitals and more. Today, Love Him Love Them continues to grow and minister to the families of Northeast Georgia and the countries of Haiti and Ukraine.

WC-193
African American Expressions is honored to work in conjunction with a wonderful non-profit organization to produce the first ever Love Him Love Them calendar for the year 2020. LHLT is a remarkable organization that exists to minister to the impoverished people of Haiti. Through the love of Jesus Christ, the founders have been able to empower those in need by building homes, churches, hospitals, and centers of education. All proceeds of this beautiful, heartening calendar directly benefit the widows and orphans under the care of Love Him Love Them.

Beauty for Ashes is a jewelry business that is run by the young ladies of Love Him Love Them Ministry with the intent of turning the recycled materials from Haiti into beautiful jewelry. With these products being handmade in Haiti from different materials, every single piece purchased is going to be special! Beauty for Ashes exists to educate, empower, and encourage these women as they transition from their current situations into becoming active members of society. By teaching the trade of jewelry making and being able to provide a living wage, we hope to encourage women and empower them to provide for their families. Our hope is to create a movement that will continue to inspire hope for their future.

These handmade items are created with limited, available materials; colors and bead size will vary.

| LHJ-01 | LHJ-02 | LHJ-03 | LHJ-04 |
| Long Necklace | Short Necklace | Earrings | Bracelet |

Love Him Love Them | **www.lovehimlovethem.org**
Give Hope, Touch Lives, Change Hearts. | Love Him Love Them is a 501(c)(3) Tax Exempt Organization.

63

Thank you to Greg Perkins and African American Expressions for the incredible Calendars you have published for Love Him Love Them and for including our Beauty for Ashes jewelry line in your international catalogue!

Thank you, Aurea McGarry, for coaching me through this process and loving our kids and dedicating your 60th birthday to us and so much more. Most of all Thank you for being my friend.

Thank you Anderson Dental Clinic for providing all the equipment for our Dental Clinic in Haiti

Thank you, Forest Padgett, and Paggett and Whetzel Family and Cosmetic Dentistry for taking care of all our kid's teeth while we were on tour. And for your pool!

Thank you to all our Mission Teams that traveled to Haiti to love on our children and help with projects and train Teachers. Thank you to all the churches that allowed us a venue to share our story.

Thank you to the volunteers that make sharing the gospel possible. The real hands and feet of Jesus.

Thank you Sarah Melco and Shirley Phillips for all the hard work you have put into baking cookies and helping with our Beauty for Ashes jewelry line. Sarah, your help with the Christmas ornaments has overwhelmed us. You are an incredibly talented and gifted woman. We are so grateful you are blessing us!

Thank you to all the Television and Radio shows that blessed us with airtime.

Producer Allison McCall and Host Benny Littlejohn with Nite Line

Dr. Trudy Simmons and The Christian View

Dorothy Spaulding and Club 36 on Watchman Broadcasting

Aurea McGarry and Jackie Arnold with Atlanta Live

HIS RADIO

FM 104 WKLY AM 980 RADIO station in Hartwell, Ga

MJ Kneiser 92.1 Lake Hartwell Radio MJ is not only the News Director at The Radio Station but also a fabulous Volunteer with Love Him Love Them.

Thank you to all our interns and Choir moms and Volunteers. We could never have done any of this without you.

Em and Haley in Haiti   Sarah in Haiti

Mommy Crystal and Daddy Chase behind the scenes on the Choir Tour

Mommy Alana our youngest Volunteer to Intern in Haiti and our Choir Mom who was Mommy Linda's right arm on the bus and so much more! We love you Mommy Alana!

Mommy Linda and Jeanna Merilien. Jeanna was scheduled to intern in Haiti and 2 days before she was to leave civil unrest hit making it unsafe for her to travel. She has traveled with the choir and much more. Thank you Jeanna Merilien for leading most amazing prayer team ever! You have a direct line to OUR FATHER and we NEED it Every Hour of every day! Jeanna is also Mommy Linda's daughter.

Thank you Kirk Franklin for loving our children and letting us sing with you so many times!

Thank you Sarah Lecroy and Barnes Academy for all you have done to make our kids dream a reality and for loving our children as if they were your very own.

Thank you to our favorite banker Esther Moulder who not only wears our Beauty for Ashes jewelry but is an amazing Volunteer and helps us with everything we do! We love you!

Thank you Olympian Naomy Grand Pierre for teaching all of our children how to swim. They all love you and imitate you every time we are in a pool.

David Gunter, Mommy Linda Mary and Todd Baxter. THANK YOU Sheriff Baxter for marrying such a beautiful and intelligent woman who knows how to get things done! We are so grateful for all you do to help us Love HIM and Love Them.

Thank you, Kelly Breymeier, for all you did to make this book a reality and for always saving my butt when I know not what to do.

*Thank you, Michael Butler, and Beyond Publishing for making all this possible
And to all the rest of you I love you! Thank you!*

Thank you most of all to these children who "gave their Lives away" to sing even when they didn't feel like it to change their lives and the lives of others forever! You are superheroes and the Hebrews 11 hall of fame of today!

Thank you Tom Martin for your help with this book and so much more and Thank you Elizabeth Thompson for your love and support and introducing me to your son.

Thank you most of all to the one who knows me best and prays for me the most and works to make us money, so I can volunteer and loves me no matter what and always has my back. I love you David.

Love,
Mommy Linda